TRUE CRIME : CONNECTICUT

D0680886

TRUE CRIME : CONNECTICUT

The State's Most Notorious Criminal Cases

Bryan Ethier

STACKPOLE
BOOKS

Published by
STACKPOLE BOOKS
5067 Ritter Road
Mechanicsburg, PA 17055
www.stackpolebooks.com

Printed in the United States of America

10 9 8 7 6 5 4 3 2 1

FIRST EDITION

Cover design by Caroline Stover

Cover photos: Handprint, ©image100/Corbis; syringe and vial, ©John Wilkes Studio/Corbis; chalk outline of body, ©Image Source/Corbis; fingerprinted paper, ©Sean Justice/Corbis

Library of Congress Cataloging-in-Publication Data

Ethier, Bryan.
    True crime : Connecticut : the state's most notorious criminal cases /
Bryan Ethier. — 1st ed.
        p.   cm.
    Includes bibliographical references.
    ISBN-13: 978-0-8117-3561-2 (pbk.)
    ISBN-10: 0-8117-3561-3 (pbk.)
    1. Crime—Connecticut. 2. Criminal investigation—Connecticut. I. Title.
HV6793.C66E84   2009
364.109746—dc22

                                                                    2008046867

Contents

Introduction

I first met Dr. Henry C. Lee in 2005, some ten years after the infamous O. J. Simpson trial. By this point, Dr. Lee was among the world's foremost forensic criminologists, and he had provided expert evidence, analysis, and testimony for some of the country's most horrific crimes, including the JonBenet Ramsey murder in 1996. My first question to Dr. Lee was one millions of people had asked a decade earlier: Had O. J. Simpson killed Nicole Brown Simpson and Ronald Goldman? Dr. Lee chuckled. He did not think Simpson had committed the crime himself, but he believed O. J. did possess the means to contract out the killing to another individual.

We spoke at length about the nature of murder—motive, means, opportunity, and so on. Our conversation eventually led to the role forensic science plays in solving crimes, especially "cold cases," those that remain unsolved and without hard leads. I concluded from our dialogue that even with the breadth of DNA testing and other high-tech analyses available to investigators, human beings still determine the relative importance of clues and the guilt or innocence of a suspect.

The murder cases chronicled in this book illustrate the many changes in crime detection over the last 170 years: the introduction of science into crime resolution; the maturation of the nation's judicial system; and fairness and honesty in the courtroom. These cases underscore the successes and failures of investigators and remind us that witnesses aren't always honest, investigators aren't always perfect, and evidence rarely lies—especially if it is "in the genes."

In the 1839 *Amistad* mutiny, murder was a heroic undertaking, used to advance the efforts of black slaves in their fight for freedom. Without the courageous efforts of one man, who knows how the course of history and slavery may have been different.

The trial following the 1878 murder of Mary Stannard highlighted the rudimentary use of forensic science in a murder investigation. The prosecution's case rested on testimony from experts on arsenic and its ability to kill a human—in this case, twenty-two-year-old Mary Stannard. The trial climaxed in a heated debate between forensic experts and a defense attorney with a keen understanding of human nature.

The creation and development of sophisticated forensic technology helped solve three other shocking cases—the 1973 murder of Concetta "Penney" Serra, the 1975 killing of Martha Moxley, and the 1986 "Wood Chipper Murder." Dr. Lee and his team of forensic science experts took police investigation into the twenty-first century, thanks to the advancement of DNA testing and more sophisticated fingerprint identification methods. Of note, the first two murders had grown cold, and remained so for years . . . until technology, and new insights from Dr. Lee, finally caught up with the crimes. Dr. Lee and his colleagues at the Connecticut State Police Forensic Science Laboratory in Meriden made national headlines in the Wood Chipper case. Their forensic evidence and crime reconstruction helped the prosecution win its case against Richard Crafts—even without the presence of a victim's body.

In 2005, serial killer Michael Ross became the state's first prisoner since 1960 to die by lethal injection. Ross's case also revealed the development of antianxiety and antidepressant drugs and their role in managing psychotic prisoners. Ross shocked the world first by confessing to the murders of eight women and then later by lobbying for his own death.

Two other homicide cases are haunting because they remind us of our own vulnerability, even in idyllic settings that seem secure. The 1998 murder of Yale University student Suzanne Jovin stunned the Yale community and virtually shattered the life of a respected instructor. Despite the evidence and testimony of witnesses, police have not arrested anyone for the crime.

In a case yet to go to trial, assailants invaded an upper-class Cheshire home, killing three family members and leaving another near death. The Petit family case not only stunned the open-door community, but also sent shock waves through the state, the legislature, and the country. If an upstanding family, beloved in its community, was wiped out, then any family could be. The prime suspects: a pair of cat burglars out on parole.

Soon after that crime, a New Britain woman lost her life during a similar home invasion. This encroachment upon the privacy and safety of homeowners did not stop there, and home invasion has become a major concern for Governor Jodi Rell. In May 2008, Rell signed into law a repeat offender bill designed to help curtail or thwart future home invasions.

CHAPTER 1
Freedom Sailors

* * *

By the mid-1990s, movie mogul Steven Spielberg had whisked movie audiences into the jaws of a great white shark and the control center of an alien spaceship. In 1997, Spielberg shifted his creative gears and escorted moviegoers on an adventure that led them from the deck of a slave ship to a Connecticut courtroom to the history books. Spielberg called his newest epic *Amistad.* For the country's most successful director and producer of commercial films, it was a vast departure from the Saturday-afternoon crowd pleasers such as the Indiana Jones series, *E.T.*, and *Jurassic Park.*

With *Amistad*, Spielberg chose to tell a story with deep social, cultural, and historical implications—a true tale of slavery, mutiny, murder, and freedom. The celluloid version of *Amistad* had a $40 million budget, and its box office receipts totaled a modest $44 million. Today, however, *Amistad* remains one of Spielberg's most important works; it is a sharp reminder of a time in a young United

States when black men, women, and children fought for the simplest of freedoms. Ultimately, *Amistad*, the movie, reintroduced the nation to a criminal case that hastened the abolition of slavery and changed the world.

As in the film, the true case of the *Amistad* began in an age when slave trading and pirating were commonplace in the United States and other countries. So was the use of slave labor, especially on southern plantations, where crop owners relied on black slaves to till and harvest their tobacco, corn, and cotton. Many U.S. businessmen bought or kidnapped their slaves from Africa, and the nautical routes between the two countries were busy from the late 1600s through the 1800s. Despite a U.S. ban on the importation of slaves that was enacted in 1808, illegal smuggling remained active.

Ship owners and other businessmen also imported African slaves to Spanish territories, such as Cuba, even though Spain had prohibited the importation of slaves since 1820. Slave traders found the Spanish treaty merely a nuisance; they beat the law by bribing officials, falsifying documents, or landing their "cargo" ships at night.

Such was the case with three Spaniards—Ramon Ferrer, Jose Ruiz, and Pedro Montes. Ferrer owned the Spanish schooner *Amistad* (*la Amistada*); Ruiz was a wealthy plantation owner; and Montes was another Spanish business mogul. In late June 1839, Ruiz and Montes went to great lengths—mostly illegal—to secure both vessel and cargo. From Ferrer, they chartered the boat; and through the usual chicanery of the times, they obtained official permits to transport the slaves from Africa to Havana.

Fifty-three slaves—most from the Mende (or Mendi) tribe of what is now Nigeria—survived a hellish journey through the Middle Passage of the Atlantic Ocean and landed at a port near Havana. Ruiz and Montes then purchased all fifty-three people, with plans to sell them to a Cuban sugar plantation. Ruiz and Montes passed off the Mendians as longtime Cuban slaves by giving them Spanish names and the designation "black landinos," symbolic of Cubans well versed in language and culture. Ruiz insured the forty-nine slaves he owned for a staggering $20,000; Montes insured for $1,300 the four children (three of them girls) he had purchased. Additionally, the traders insured for $40,000 a cargo that included a wealth of jewelry and other personal luxury items.

The *Amistad* set sail on June 28, 1839, with Ferrer at the helm and fifty-three slaves, a crew of five, and Montes and Ruiz on board. Little did Montes and Ruiz know what would soon befall them—a mutiny of historic proportion.

The trip from Havana to Puerto Principe typically took three days, but strong winds slowed the schooner, extending the voyage by one more fateful day. On the fourth night at sea, the Mendians began their revolt, engineered by the tribe's leader, Sengbe-Pieh, a farmer who was rumored to be the son of a local Mende chief. Sengbe used a spike he had pried from the deck to unshackle himself and the other slaves.

For more than seventy-two hours, the Mende slaves had been whipped and tormented; at one point, one crewmember had threatened to chop them into pieces and cook their remains for supper. Now, with freedom in their grasp, they plotted the overthrow of the crew and captain. Sengbe and others secreted sugar cane knives captured from the cargo hold. Then they waited for morning.

At dawn, the Africans stole their way onto the deck, led by Sengbe. In the ensuing pandemonium, Sengbe sliced Ferrer's throat, killed the cook, and seriously wounded Montes. Two of the Mendians died in the attack, and two white seamen escaped from the *Amistad* in a small boat. With the schooner under his control, Sengbe turned his attention to the traders. Although the tribal leader had the wherewithal to overthrow the Spaniards, he had no experience navigating a ship. With Ferrer, the captain, dead, Sengbe had little choice but to spare the lives of the two other Spaniards. He ordered them to navigate the vessel back to Africa.

Montes, a former sailor, had modest sailing skills. He also had no intention of navigating the ship to Africa—and an uncertain fate. Using the stars as a guide, Montes steered the *Amistad* east toward

Africa during the day; at night, he reversed his course toward the United States, hoping to land at a sympathetic Cuban port. The schooner continued on a zigzag course for two months. During that time, the crew exhausted its rations, and eight more slaves died from dehydration and exposure to the elements. Despite the constant peril and brutal hardship, Sengbe maintained control over the ship and, for the most part, over the Spaniards.

In late August 1839, the *Amistad* drifted to the shores of Long Island, New York. Sengbe and others went ashore seeking food, supplies, and help back to Africa from local seamen. Not surprisingly, the locals who encountered the Mende slaves gaped at their visitors and their unusual appearance and requests. Two sea captains, Peletiah Fordham and Henry Green, were engaged in a relaxing day of bird shooting when four black men, wearing only blankets, approached them. The sailors used sign language to assure the Mendians that they were not in slaveholding territory and thus in no danger. Reassured, the Mendians led Fordham and Green to a spot on the sand dunes that commanded a clear view of the stark black schooner, its sails shredded, anchored less than a mile from shore. From there, Fordham and Green also spotted a smaller boat on the beach, manned by other black men wearing gold necklaces and bracelets. One of the Mendians (it is unclear whether it was Sengbe) offered the sailors two trunks filled with gold if they would provide the crew with provisions and sail them back to Africa. Green, his mind wild with visions of prosperity, intimated that they could forge a deal, if they received the gold.

For both slaves and seamen, this was a no-lose proposition . . . except for one thing. By now, word had spread through the local newspapers about the strange black schooner that seemed to circle aimlessly around the Long Island shoreline. Rumors of the slaves' revolt—and the fortune on deck—also reached the sea. As luck would have it, a U.S. Coast Guard brig named *Washington* cut off the rowboat as it headed back to the *Amistad*. Lieutenant Thomas Gedney, the ship's commander, boarded the schooner and ordered all men below deck.

Ruiz and Montes, who remained under Sengbe's control, saw the arrival of the *Washington* as their one chance for freedom. Montes, weak, pallid, and sobbing, emerged from below deck, begging Gedney for help. Ruiz, who was in his mid-twenties, made a far more presentable picture. He appealed to Gedney's sense of propriety and recounted a blood-chilling story of murder, treachery, and mutiny aboard the *Amistad*. Ruiz neglected to disclose, however, that the Mendians had been brought illegally from Africa to Cuba, defying the treaty between Spain and Britain that prohibited the importation of slaves to Spanish colonies.

As Ruiz regaled Gedney with the "facts of the mutiny," Sengbe raced from below decks, naked except for a gold necklace. Sengbe was a powerfully built man, and a strong swimmer since his youth. Before Gedney or the other members of the crew could react, Sengbe sped off and dived from the ship. The *Washington* gave chase, but its power—initially—was no match for the man's athleticism and elusiveness. When the man finally tired, he dropped the priceless necklace to the bottom of the sea and continued to swim. Eventually, however, crewmembers recaptured Sengbe and put him in shackles.

On August 26, Gedney took control of the *Amistad* and had it towed to New London, Connecticut. News quickly spread of the slaves' capture. The New London *Gazette* was one of the first newspapers to shed light on the mutiny of the Mende and the murder of the crewmembers:

TUESDAY, 12 o'clock, M.

We have just returned from a visit to the *Washington* and her prize, which are riding at anchor in the bay, near the fort. On board the former we saw and conversed with the two Spanish gentlemen who were passengers on board the schooner, as well as owners of the Negroes and most of the cargo.

One of them, Jose Rues [*sic*], is very gentlemanly and intelligent young man, and speaks English fluently. He was the owner of most of the slaves and cargo, which he was conveying to his estate on the Island of Cuba.

The other, Pedro Montes, is about fifty years of age, and is the owner of three slaves. He was formerly a ship-master, and has navigated the vessel since her seizure by the blacks. Both of them, as may be naturally supposed are most unfeignedly thankful for their deliverance. Signor Pedro is the most striking instance of complacency and unalloyed delight we ever have seen, and it is not strange, since only yesterday his sentence was pronounced by the chief of the buccaneers, and his death song chanted by the grim crew, who gathered with uplifted sabres around his devoted head, which, as well as his arms, bear the scars of several wounds inflicted at the time of the murder of the ill-fated captain and crew.

He sat smoking his Havana on the deck, and, to junge [*sic*] from the martyr-like serenity of his countenance, his emotions are such as rarely stir the heart of man. When Mr. Porter, the prize-master, assured him of his safety, he threw his arms around his neck, while gushing tears coursing down his furrowed cheek, bespoke the overflowing transport of his soul. Every now and then he clasps his hands, and with uplifted eyes gives thanks to "the Holy Virgin" who had led him out of all his troubles.

Senor Rues [*sic*] has given us two letters for his agents, Messrs, Shelton, Brothers & Co., of Boston, and Peter A. Harmony & Co., of New York. It appears that the slaves, the greater portion of whom were his, were very much attached to him, and had determined, after reaching the coast of Africa, to allow him to seek his home what way he could, while his poor companion was to be sacrificed.

On board the brig we also saw [Sengbe], the master-spirit and hero of this bloody tragedy, in irons. He is about five feet eight inches in height, 25 or 26 years of age, of erect figure, well built, and very active. He is said to be a match for any two men on board the schooner. His countenance, for a native African, is unusually intelligent, evincing uncommon decision and coolness, with a composure characteristic of true courage and nothing to mark him as a malicious man. He is a Negro who would command, in New Orleans, under the hammer, at least $1,500.

He is said to have killed the captain and crew with his own hand, by cutting their throats. He also has several times attempted to take the life of Senor Montes [Montez], and the backs of several poor Negroes are scored with the scars of blows inflicted by his lash to keep them in submission. He expects to be executed, but nevertheless manifests a sang froid worthy of a Sto[ne] under similar circumstances.

With Capt. Gedney, the surgeon of the port, and others, we visited the schooner, which is anchored within musket shot of the *Washington*, and there we saw such a sight as we never saw before, and never wish to see again. The bottom and sides of this vessel are covered with barnacles and sea-grass, while her rigging and sales [*sic*] present a scene worthy of the Flying Dutchman, after her fabled cruise. She is a Baltimore built vessel of matchless model for speed, about 120 tons burthen and about six years old.

On her deck were grouped, amid various goods and arms, the remnant of her Ethiop[ian] crew, some decked in the most fantastic manner in the silks and finery pilfered from the cargo while others, in a state of nudity, emaciated to mere skeletons, lay coiled upon the decks. Here could be seen a negro with white pantaloons and the sable shirt which nature gave him, and a planter's broad-brimmed hat upon his head, with a string of gewgaws around his neck; and another with a linen cambric shirt, whose bosom was worked by the hand of some dark-eyed daughter of Spain, while his nether proportions were enveloped in a shawl of gauze and Canton crape. Around the windlass were gathered the three little girls, from eight to thirteen years of age, the very images of health and gladness.

Over the deck were scattered, in the most wanton and disorderly profusion, raisins, vermicelli, bread, rice, silk, and cotton goods. In the cabin and hold were the marks of the same wasteful destruction—Her cargo appears to consist of silks, crapes, calicoes, cotton and fancy goods of various descriptions, glass and hardware, bridles, saddles, holsters, pictures, looking-glasses, books, fruits, olives, and olive oil, and "other things too numerous to mention," which are now all mixed up in a strange and fantastic medldy [*sic*].

On the forward hatch we unconsciously rested our hand on a cold object, which we soon discovered to be a naked corpse enveloped in a pall of black bombazine. On removing its folds we beheld the rigid countenance and glazed eye of a poor Negro who died last night. His mouth was unclosed, and still wore the ghastly expression of his last struggle. Near by him, like some watching fiend, sat the most horrible creature we ever saw in human shape, an object of terror to the very blacks, who said that he was a cannibal. His teeth projected at almost right angles from his mouth, while his eyes had a most savage and demoniac expression.

When the ship arrived the following day, Gedney contacted the U.S. marshal at New Haven, who then notified U.S. District Judge Andrew Judson. Judson's reputation was renowned in the state; in 1833, he had prosecuted a woman for accepting blacks into her school in Canterbury. Still, it was uncertain whether any crimes had been committed on the schooner, or if U.S. courts had jurisdiction over the matter. With the future of the kidnapped slaves at stake, Judge Judson held court on board the *Washington* two days later, with Montes and Ruiz providing details of their sixty-three harrowing days at sea under the control of Sengbe and the other Mendians.

Ruiz testified: "I took an oar and tried to quell the mutiny. I cried 'No! No!' I then heard one of the crew cry murder. I then heard the captain order the cabin boy to go below and get some bread to throw among the Negroes, hoping to pacify them. I did not see the captain killed."

Montes also chronicled the Africans' uprising on the fourth night at sea: "Between three and four was awakened by a noise which was caused by blows to the mulatto cook. I went on deck and they attacked me. I seized a stick and a knife with a view to defend myself . . . At this time [Sengbe] wounded me on the head severely with one of the sugar knives, also on the arm. I then ran below and stowed myself between two barrels, wrapped up in a sail. [Sengbe] rushed after me and attempted to kill me, but was prevented by the interference of another man . . . I was then taken on deck and tied to the hand of Ruiz."

Now confident of their safety, and the case against Sengbe and the others, Montes and Ruiz demanded the surrender of the slaves and the cargo to the Spanish consul in Boston. Judson reviewed the testimonies and then released the two Spaniards. He ordered the slaves tried for murder and piracy, setting a trial date for September 17 in Hartford Circuit Court. He dispatched the Africans to a county jail in New Haven.

Ruiz, meanwhile, further solidified the case against Sengbe by renaming him Jose Cinque, a rough Spanish translation of Sengbe. Ruiz hoped to show that Cinque was not a recently imported slave and that he, Ruiz, was not guilty of breaking the 1820 Spanish slave probation treaty.

The "facts" and the odds were stacked against the Mendians as they awaited their trial. In the time before the *Amistad* Africans awaited their fate, nearly 12 million blacks had been "shepherded" to North and South America. White southern plantation owners maintained control over the slave trade industry, and they filled their coffers with coins garnered primarily from slave labor on their plantations. Meanwhile, as some southern slaveowners transported their slaves by boat—with Norfolk to New Orleans a common route—many business owners forced their indentured blacks to walk on death marches. Some slaves chose flight—and likely capture and death—over servitude. Some died during the grueling marches. Those that survived the journey faced bleak futures in compounds barely more survivable than the Nazi death camps of World War II.

Those slaves pirated from Africa were tortured on the trip to North America. They were bound in couples, their arms and legs shackled both day and night. With the space between decks no taller than four feet, the slaves were forced to crouch, if they were bold enough to attempt to stand. The decks were teeming with captives. There was rice in abundance, but little to drink. Deck hands whipped those who did not finish their meals, and some slaves—ill or other-wise—ate under duress until they vomited. Many died before reaching the ship's destination.

Economically, the United States was headed toward an industrial boom, while small antislavery groups were starting to sprout around the country. The press had begun to chronicle the hellish existence of the slaves. The *Amistad* case would help meld these loosely-formed splinter groups in their efforts to abolish slavery. The first step was freeing Sengbe and the other imprisoned Africans.

Hours after Judson had consigned the slaves to the New Haven jail, the town's abolitionists sought the assistance of fellow anti-slavery advocates in New York. They requested help in verifying the ship's documents and in obtaining legal counsel for the Mendians. Because the Africans neither spoke nor understood English, the local abolitionists asked the New York group to find a translator to record the slaves' accounts of what had happened at sea.

In September, one abolitionist, Lewis Tappan, formed a committee to defend the Africans. He called the group the Friends of Amistad Africans Committee. Headed by wealthy New York merchants and well-known abolitionists, the committee began its defense of Sengbe and the other Mendians by appealing to the community. In a letter penned by colleagues Simeon S. Jocelyn, Joshua Leavitt, and Tappan, the abolitionists called upon freedom fighters to donate money and clothing to the bereft slaves. They said the slaves had been "piratically kidnapped from their own land, transported across the sea, and subjected to atrocious cruelties." The community, the state, and the country would soon learn the details of those atrocities from the testimonies of Sengbe and others.

The route to freeing the *Amistad* slaves was a long and treacherous one, but the committee had taken the first important step—bringing the case to the attention of the nation.

The committee then created a "dream team," consisting of renowned attorneys Roger Baldwin, Seth Staple, and Theodore Sedgwick, to represent the slaves. Yet these men of fine minds and strategy still lacked one important asset: understanding of the Mendian language. The lawyers recognized that without direct testimony from Sengbe and the others, they would have little chance of winning the trial. With Tappan as the vanguard, the committee brought in from New York three Africans, one of whom had limited knowledge of the Mendian language. This interpreter held interviews with the captives and gleaned enough information to validate the opinions of the committee: the *Amistad* slaves had been kidnapped, and thus sold illegally into slavery.

On September 17, all but one slave, who was too ill to attend, appeared in Hartford Circuit Court, with Judge Smith Thompson presiding. For three days, Thompson heard testimony from a number of witnesses and experts as his courtroom turned into a hall for an unprecedented debate over freedom. Finally, Thompson ruled that a circuit court had "no jurisdiction over the charges of murder and piracy, since the alleged crimes were committed on a Spanish ship and Spanish waters." All claims over the slaves and cargo on the ship should be settled in a district court, Thompson added. The slaves returned to jail, and both sides of the case prepared for their next battle.

The respite gave the committee the opportunity to steel its defense, and its first order of business was acquiring an interpreter who was fluent in the Mendian language. This time luck was on its side. J. W. Gibbs, professor of theology and sacred literature at Yale Divinity School, was one of the many locals interested in both the case and the Mendians. Since the imprisonment of the slaves, Gibbs had learned to count from one to ten in their language. Wishing to help the slaves in any way possible, Gibbs ventured to the docks of New York in search of an interpreter. As sailors emerged from their ships, Gibbs counted in Mende, hoping someone would recognize the language.

Finally, in early October, Gibbs's efforts paid off when he found British sailor James Covey aboard the warship *Buzzard*. Covey recognized Gibbs's counting; he was a Mendian who had been captured as a child. He was later recaptured by the British and joined the British Navy when he came of age. Now he was about to become the mouthpiece for a historic judgement on the institution of slavery.

Covey accompanied Gibbs to New Haven; he received a rousing chorus of cheers from the slaves, who realized they would finally get their story told.

The nation did not yet know the history of the slaves and their journey aboard the *Amistad*, but the townspeople in New Haven and its environs were curious about them. Some visitors paid 12$1/2$ cents to visit the slaves. The committee realized that the captives had become part of a bizarre sideshow tantamount to a traveling circus. By this time, several Mendians had died from the effects of dehydration, hunger, and exposure. Seeking to improve their living conditions, the Amistad Committee employed Reverend George Day, a former employee at the New York School for the Deaf and Dumb, to supervise the religious, social, and academic instruction of the slaves by Yale Divinity School students. The teachers used simple sign language and rudimentary pictures to help bridge the vast communication gap.

Despite these improvements in the slaves' welfare and growing sympathy for their plight, their release remained a long shot. Pressure on federal, state, and local courts to convict the slaves mounted.

Meanwhile, Spain continued to fight for custody of the slaves and the ship's expensive cargo. Spanish Minister Frances Calderon de la Barca wrote to U.S. Secretary of State John Forsyth that when "the *Amistad* was rescued, it should have been set free to return to Cuba so that the Africans on board could have been tried by the proper tribunal, and by the violated laws of the country of which they are subjects." Moreover, he claimed the schooner and its cargo in the name of the Spanish monarch and demanded they be returned to Havana for arbitration.

While international pressure mounted, U.S. President Martin Van Buren pondered the dilemma the *Amistad* slaves posed. The president was publicly neither for nor against slavery; but he did know that without the backing of powerful Southern Democrats, his bid for reelection in 1840 might fail. Slave labor was good for business, the southern economy, and the future of the country. Cost-free labor increased the gross profits of the southern businesses, and dollars meant Democratic votes to Van Buren.

Van Buren hardly needed a group of abolitionists and a high-profile trial to bolster the abolitionist movement and build additional national sympathy for slaves. The trial, the *Amistad* slaves, and the media attention had to go away, Van Buren mused. And "away" meant back to Cuba for Sengbe and the other captives. The president garnered much-needed support from U.S. Attorney General Felix Grundy, who declared the slaves to be Spanish property. He recommended that the ship and its cargo return to Cuba immediately; the cabinet concurred.

The Amistad Committee remained upbeat and undaunted in its mission to free the slaves, despite Van Buren's pressure and efforts to extradite the Mendians. The committee built a defense strategy on the premise that the African captives were not legally slaves. The captives had been brought to Havana and sold there in violation of the Anglo-Spanish treaty of 1820, which prohibited transatlantic slave trade.

Testimony from Dr. R. R. Madden also bolstered the committee's argument. Madden had served the British government in Ghana and Havana as a commissioner on the Court of Mixed Commission for Suppressing the Slave Trade. Madden disclosed that the Spanish captain-general and other officials had sanctioned the violation of the slave trade treaty numerous times. Furthermore, Madden claimed that Nicholas Trist, American consul in Cuba, had collaborated and reaped "huge financial benefits" from illegal slave trade.

In November, Madden came to New York and discussed these implications with Tappan. Madden also met with the captives, and he gave testimony to Judge Judson in chambers. He argued that the African slaves were "recent importees," and that papers of ownership possessed by Ruiz and Montes were not legally valid.

At about this same time, Montes and Ruiz were arrested in New York on charges of assault, kidnapping, and false imprisonment, rendered by two of the Africans. Montes quickly paid the $1,000 bail and fled for Cuba. Ruiz chose to remain in jail, seek the support of the public, and build public opinion against the *Amistad* slaves. The committee, now led vigorously by Tappan, refused to succumb. Ruiz, after a while, grew tired of jail, paid bail, and returned to Cuba. Neither man appeared at the final hearing.

On November 19, 1839, the U.S. District Court of Hartford opened to hear the *Amistad* case. When key witnesses were not available for the trial, however, the case was adjourned until January 1840.

Van Buren, meanwhile, still sought a quick, clean conclusion to the *Amistad* affair. With the Spanish minister continuing to pressure for the release of the cargo, Forsyth made plans for a vessel to return the captives to Cuba, should the verdict go against them. On January 8, the U.S. Navy schooner *Grampus* stood in New Haven Harbor, under the directive of Van Buren. The president's direct efforts to thwart justice sparked further outcries from the public. The Amistad Committee, sensing Van Buren's desperation, established a team to keep watch over the slaves around the clock. They feared that the president might send men to seize the slaves before the completion of the trial. Tappan and his colleagues even considered hiding the Africans.

When the case went to trial, it was not the Amistad Committee's dream team that swayed the decision in favor of the Africans, but the testimony of Sengbe. Through the interpreter, Covey, Sengbe gave a stirring firsthand account of the slaves' kidnapping and physical and mental abuse. As the trial drew to a stunning climax, Sengbe stood and bellowed in English, "Give us free! Give us free!"

On January 13, 1840, Judge Judson delivered his verdict: The Africans had been kidnapped and sold into slavery illegally, in violation of Spanish law. They were to be released and returned to their native country.

Judson's verdict should have sealed the case. But his decision did not reflect the sentiment of most Americans—including President Martin Van Buren. Shortly after Judson had declared the slaves free, Van Buren ordered District Attorney William S. Holabird to appeal the decision. The *Amistad* slaves returned to jail, their future once again in peril.

Van Buren's meddling did not escape the attention of the press. On February 10, the *Hartford Courant* published an article that was highly critical of the president's involvement in the *Amistad* case:

We are informed by a gentleman from New Haven that a short time previous to the trial of the Africans of the *Amistad*, before the U.S. District Court at New Haven, Judge Judson presiding, Martin Van Buren addressed a letter to the judge recommending and urging him to order the Africans to be taken back to Havana in a government vessel, to be sold there as slaves . . .

The letter of the President, recommending that these poor unfortunate Africans be sent into perpetual bondage, is said to contain statements disgraceful to the high station of its author, and which, were they published, would excite the indignation of every Republican freeman in the land. What will the friends of liberty say to this? Surely, Martin Van Buren is playing the part of a tyrant with a high hand—else why this tampering with our courts of justice, this Executive usurpation, and this heartless violation of the inalienable rights of man? Of the truth of the above, there is no doubt, and we leave the unprincipled author of such a proceeding in the hands of a just and highly-minded People.

Despite their disappointment at the outcome of the trial, the Africans continued their education. Although incarcerated physically, the slaves could still grow spiritually and intellectually, thanks to their schooling. Covey taught them English and translated Christian prayers into Mende. The slaves approached their studies with vigor and discipline, devouring each lesson taught by the Yale Divinity School teachers.

By the fall of 1840, the Mendians had gained in education and amalgamation, but the committee lacked political might. Tappan and his colleagues recognized that they needed a titan to counter Van Buren in the political arena. In October, after failing to hire a number of lawyers, the committee turned to former president John Quincy Adams to lead their defense. Adams had not practiced law in some thirty years, and he was approaching his seventy-fourth birthday. Still, he had publicly expressed an interest in the slaves and the trial.

In October, Adams visited the surviving *Amistad* Africans in their jail in Westville, a suburb of New Haven. What the former president

WELCOME HOME, *AMISTAD*

On December 9, 2007, William Pinkney celebrated freedom as few have in the last two hundred years. On that historic day, Pinkney, the master emeritus of the schooner *Amistad*, steered the 129-foot ship to the dock of Freetown, the capital of Sierra Leone. Pinkney, maritime consultant Merle Smith, and Captain Eliza Garfield received a hero's welcome and shouts of "*Amistad*! Freedom!" from thousands of Sierra Leoneans on hand.

It was a moment Pinkney said he would never forget. "I had hoped I'd be around long enough to do this," Pinkney told the *New Haven Register*.

Captained by Garfield, the schooner had traversed seven thousand miles in just under six months at sea. This was the first leg of a voyage scheduled to conclude in New Haven in August 2008. The voyage was part of the Atlantic Freedom Tour, commemorating the two hundredth anniversary of the abolition of Atlantic slave trade in the British Empire. The docking of the *Amistad* in Sierra Leone was a poignant reminder of arguably the most important battle for freedom in the history of the country.

saw further encouraged him to take action: Sengbe and the other slaves were packed into one room, thirty by twenty feet. Cots, thirty-six all told, filled nearly every inch of floor space. Sengbe and Grabeau, another captive, greeted Adams and spoke with him at length. Said Adams, "God willing, we will make you free."

In what was later termed the "trial of one president by another," Attorney Roger Baldwin prepared a detailed, airtight defense and opened the case impressively. His address, however, paled in comparison to the rousing eloquence of Adams's four-and-a-half-hour speech to the court on February 24. "Old Man Eloquent," as Adams was popularly known, still enjoyed the power to persuade, despite his frailty. He argued that if Van Buren had the power to send the Africans to Cuba, he would equally enjoy the freedom to send them overseas for a trial. Adams argued that Spain was requesting the

Pinkney first learned of the *Amistad* in 1976 from Warren Q. Marr II of the NAACP. Marr envisioned the building of a replica of the schooner to help introduce the story to those living today. The *Amistad* on which Pinkney sailed was the second replica of the original ship. Launched in 2000, it calls New Haven its home port.

Pinkney and Marr shared the realization of a passionate dream when the ship docked in Africa. "I carried all of those [slaves] with me when I came to that dock," said Pinkney. "It was just overwhelming. I felt that I was home. Being of African descent, I still do not know what tribe or nation I came from. I felt I had an opportunity to choose my native home, so I chose Sierra Leone."

The "return" of the *Amistad* to its African home also served as a symbol of how precious freedom tastes to the Sierra Leoneans. In July 2006, the country elected a new government to power after years of civil war. The arrival of the *Amistad* was a poignant reminder of how far this nation has come to establish peace and freedom for all.

American president to "first turn man-robber . . . next turn jailer . . . and lastly turn catchpole and convey them to Havana, to appease the vengeance of the African slave traders of the barracoons." On March 9, 1841, the Supreme Court issued its final verdict regarding the "kidnapped Africans, who by the laws of Spain itself were entitled to their freedom." The *Amistad* slaves were free.

Adams capped the momentous decision with a brief letter to Tappan: "Thanks—Thanks in the name of humanity and justice to YOU."

Despite the victory, the Mendians would not return to their homeland for some time. Van Buren remained bitter in defeat, denying them free transport to Sierra Leone. Released from custody, the slaves returned to Farmington, one of the state's first abolitionist towns. There they continued their education. To raise funds needed to charter a boat, the Africans embarked on a speaking tour throughout the northern states. By this time, Sengbe—or "Joseph Cinque," as he was nationally known—was an icon, compared by newspapers to "heroes of ancient Greece and Rome." Sengbe transfixed his audiences with details of the Africans' ordeals—all imparted in flawless English.

Finally, by the end of 1841, the committee had raised enough money to charter the barque *Gentleman*. The thirty-five surviving Mendians, accompanied by five American missionaries (including two teachers), returned to Sierra Leone, instructed by the committee to establish a Mende mission. Within three years, American missionary activity had begun in the area. In time, the American Missionary Association transferred its mission posts in Sierra Leone to the United Brethren in Christ (UBC). UBC not only was responsible for local evangelical work, it also developed a broad system of mission schools in the southern part of the country. Also, many of the students who studied in the American mission schools in Sierra Leone relocated to the United States to further their education. A new relationship between the United States and Africa had been formed—one based on Christian principles instead of slavery.

At home, the *Amistad* case set in motion the conditions that would eventually lead to the abolition of slavery. Initially, the freeing of the thirty-five Africans further alienated the antislavery North and slaveholding South. Emboldened by the successful conclusion of the case, abolitionist groups continued to grow in number and power. Still, southern business leaders and politicians fought to maintain their businesses with slave labor. Eventually, the contentious battle over slavery became one of the components that led to the Civil War in 1861. Often overlooked in this political and cultural war was the role the American Missionary Association (AMA) played in leading to the eventual prohibition of slavery. Spawned from the *Amistad* case and the plight of many of the African slaves, the AMA became one of the most powerful antislavery groups in America.

In the end, the heroic efforts of Sengbe and the other captives aboard the *Amistad* did not abolish slavery, but they helped eliminate some of the barriers that prevented all men from being equal.

CHAPTER 2

Arsenic and Murder

***

It is the late nineteenth century, the Victorian era. Women are second-class citizens, practically mute in their opinions. Abortion is illegal, and women who bear children out of wedlock are social pariahs, condemned and often isolated by society. To the callous young men so imprudent to leave them with child, these women are "inconveniences."

Crime detection is equally primitive, and the administration of justice rarely objective, accurate, and equitable. Police, witnesses, and the curious often compromise crime scenes. In the courtroom, witnesses' statements frequently waver according to their prejudices and to suit the individual cases. Attorneys often use "discretionary truth" when the prosecution represents a woman and the defense a man.

The press, meanwhile, posts the facts from time to time, but almost as frequently publishes rumor, scandal, and speculation as truth. Reporters often not only color the proceedings of trials with

19

their own perspective, but also add their opinions to their stories. Prospective jurors, reading this "yellow journalism," often change their minds about the guilt or innocence of the accused.

The press is more than a purveyor of news and gossip; it also is an investigative arm of many local police departments. If investigators are slow afoot to solve a crime, reporters are eager muckrakers, often a step ahead of the men with badges. Truth may be the goal of investigators, but for newspapers, outscooping the others with the latest news is the prize. Banner headlines yield greater sales, and newsmen often conduct their own investigations. Truth is in the eyes—and pencil—of the beholder.

In this arbitrary, prejudiced world, Mary Stannard lived—and consequently died before her time. Admired by many of her neighbors and the community, she nevertheless was a woman of imperfections, flaws which ultimately proved fatal. Mary Stannard was an inconvenience in a world that rarely forgave such marked women. Her death in 1878 through arsenic poisoning shocked the state, made banner headlines, and introduced the courtroom to forensic science as a means of proving guilt or innocence. Experts in arsenic descended upon New Haven County to produce some of the most mind-boggling and advanced testimony of its time.

In the main, twenty-two-year-old Mary Stannard was a solid, respected member of the Madison community. She worked hard, not only at home, but also as a domestic to some of her neighbors. Her employers, family, and friends lauded her honesty, and she was always ready to lend a hand to a neighbor in need. Children especially adored Stannard, and she often cared for them both on the job and at home.

Like many people in the Victorian era, Mary received little education and was barely literate. She was from a poor family; her father, Charles, was an illiterate farmer who earned scant money, mostly from occasional odd jobs. Stannard's half sister, Susan Hawley, remained at home and performed the domestic duties. The two young women were close, dependent on each other in many ways.

Susan, for instance, often cared for Stannard's two-year-old son, Willie, who was dubbed "the bastard" in certain quarters.

Mary Stannard was, in nineteenth-century terms, simple—naïve in today's vernacular—especially concerning men and romance. She was neither chaste nor lascivious, but desperately yearned to start her own family. Such a deep-seated need manifested in a vulnerability that attracted dishonorable men to her bedroom. Already her eager innocence had betrayed her. In the summer of 1875, Mary was working as a domestic for a family in Northford. In the family was a young married man taken to flirting with Mary. Socially, she was inferior to the educated suitor. Still, her naïveté charmed the man, while her desperation to belong to a family encouraged him to pursue her sexually. Willie was born the following April; Mary Stannard was just nineteen years old at the time.

Usually, anyone in Stannard's position would be run out of town. Mary Stannard's case was different, however. So respected was she in her community that her neighbors broke tradition by forgiving this one transgression. Still, even the magnanimous folks in Madison did not forgive such an error twice. Neither did Reverend Herbert H. Hayden.

If Mary Stannard spun dreams of creating her own family, Reverend Hayden held big plans for his life at the altar. He preached at a Methodist church in Madison but longed to be an ordained minister. He was a man with big dreams and big goals, but God had neither blessed him with a sharp academic mind, the necessary finances, nor life's good timing to transform his dreams into reality.

Hayden was working toward a degree at Wesleyan University that would help him become ordained into the Methodist ministry when his wife, Rosa, gave birth to their first child, Emma. Rosa, a teacher, had had a difficult childbirth, and the birth of their second child, Herbert Leonard, was equally difficult—so difficult that Rosa needed help caring for their children while her husband was away preaching. By that time, Reverend Hayden had garnered a teaching job in Madison, a few miles from their home in Rockland, and he stayed in the town where he taught throughout the workweek. The Haydens needed help for the ailing Rosa, who could not bear to be alone while her husband was away.

Enter Mary Stannard, who worked and stayed in the Hayden home during the reverend's absences. Mary was more than a domestic to the family; she was a companion to Rosa Hayden. When Reverend Hayden returned on Friday evenings, Mary made the short walk back to the Stannard home, less than a mile away.

The arrangement benefited all and ran smoothly until December 1877, when Rosa discovered the source of her malaise: She was pregnant once again. Hayden did not receive the news gladly; their household was large enough, and money was scarce. The last thing Reverend Herbert H. Hayden needed was another mouth to feed. Hayden already had turned to friends for cash loans, including a $75 note from Susan Hawley. Hayden, as his benefactors noted sourly, was not in the habit of repaying loans.

By March 1878, Hayden's world was beginning to crumble around his feet. Rosa was well into her pregnancy, the family was nearly broke, and his dream of becoming an ordained minister was fading. Hayden needed something—or someone—to stabilize his life, even if briefly. He turned to Mary Stannard to be his emotional lifeboat. At the time when Mary had entered the Hayden household, sex between Rosa and Herbert was rare. Then again, in Victorian America, sex was considered predominantly a tool for procreation, not a source of pleasure. Mary Stannard, however, was young, vital, attractive, and most important, vulnerable to a man's charm . . . a stationary object in the reverend's world, which was spinning wildly out of his control. Slowly the reverend began to exert his will—and charm—over his wistful domestic.

Finally, on the night of the town oyster festival, Reverend Herbert Hayden made a decision that would forever change his life. As was the norm, Mary was at the Hayden house, caring for the children. At 10 P.M., Hayden told Rosa that he was not feeling well; he would rush home from the festival to take some medicine and then return in a short while, when he felt better. Rosa asked him if he could check on the children. Hayden had little doubt that the children were asleep; that left Mary alone, subject to his wily ways.

Hayden was not an unattractive man—slightly stocky, neatly dressed and groomed—and many townspeople speculated that he'd wooed more than one young lady in recent years. Mary Stannard, so wanting, would be easy prey. After all, hadn't another man taken her to his bed before?

Hayden returned to a house in order; quiet, and with Mary resting in the sitting room. What followed immediately was predictable.

That the reverend was a "man of God" was moot in relation to Mary Stannard. The pair enjoyed a tryst that was hardly private. No one publicly questioned the relationship; after all, who would question the veracity of said man of God? Hayden continued to preach; Rosa remained at home, expecting her third child.

Like most affairs, the relationship between preacher and domestic ran its course. By August, the Haydens had welcomed their child into the world, and Mary Stannard had moved on to work for another family, the Studleys of Guilford. Life was pleasant for Mary, the relationship with Hayden relegated to memory. For a while, at least.

Then the vomiting began. And her breasts began to swell. And Mary Stannard was scared.

During a bout of heaving in the Studleys' privy, Mary Stannard came face-to-face with an ugly, frightening truth: She was pregnant again. This time the Reverend Herbert Hayden was the father. Mary understood the repercussions of bearing another child out of wedlock. There would be no forgiveness this time.

Panic-stricken, on August 29 she confided in Jane Studley, her employer. Mary told her everything, shaken, weeping, fearful of the future. Mrs. Studley was a sturdy, emotionally strong woman in her sixties. She took Mary aside and examined her thoroughly. Did she feel a lump in Mary's abdomen? Possibly. And what of Mary's menstrual cycle?

Mary admitted that, yes, she still had her menstrual period; but she'd known other women to spot during pregnancy. Based on her examination of the girl, Mrs. Studley wasn't convinced that Mary Stannard was pregnant.

Had Stannard lived in contemporary times, she would have consulted a gynecologist to confirm the pregnancy. But she did not have enough money to pay for a medical exam, and she certainly could not afford an abortion. Her solution to the problem reflected the culture of the day: Herbert Hayden would pay to make this problem go away.

On August 30, Mary wrote two letters. The first was to Reverend Hayden, fully disclosing her apparent pregnancy and requesting his help. The second was to her father. On the back side of the letter to Charles Stannard, Mary wrote a short note to her half sister, Susan, asking her not to read the confidential letter to the reverend. She signed both letters—barely literate—with a shaking hand, and then asked the Studleys' son Edgar to mail the letter for her.

The writing was cathartic, and Mary felt a sense of hope. That flicker of hope died quickly when the senior Studley learned of Mary's "inconvenience." He would not have a woman of that nature under his roof. She and her "bastard child" Willie, who often stayed with his mother at the Studleys' home, would have to leave.

With little recourse, mother and son left the Studleys' employment and returned to the Stannard home in Madison. Susan Hawley was quick to suspect by her sister's sullen demeanor that something was wrong. Susan questioned Mary until her sister burst into tears with the truth about her pregnancy and Reverend Hayden. As they were talking, Charles Hawley (Susan's brother) and his wife, also named Mary, entered the room bearing the letters Mary Stannard had written. Susan saw the envelope with the name "Mr. Hayden" written on it. She reached for the envelope, but her sister was too quick. No one, vowed Mary Stannard, would ever know the contents of the letter.

Little did she know that had a jury later been granted access to the information therein, the outcome of the Great Case might have been different . . .

On September 2, Mary Stannard gathered all of her courage and traveled to the Hayden home, ostensibly to borrow a pitchfork for her father. It took her two subsequent trips to find Reverend Hayden at home. At 4 P.M. that day, she and the reverend stole away to the barn to retrieve the tool. During the later trial, members of Hayden's family denied such a meeting; other witnesses confirmed it, however.

Hayden agreed to help Mary. He either would purchase medicine from a drugstore in Middletown to abort the child or would contact a doctor to perform an abortion, though it was illegal in the nineteenth century. Either way, thought Mary, her problems were solved.

On Tuesday, September 3, Mary Stannard turned twenty-two. Wearing her best calico dress, she celebrated her birthday surrounded by her family and their longtime friend, Ben Stevens. Stevens, their sixty-two-year-old neighbor, had been a widower for years and had adopted the Stannards as a surrogate family. In fact, Susan Hawley had helped Stevens care for his mother during her dying days three years earlier.

Early that morning, Mary retrieved two of the Hayden children, Emmie and Lennie, and spent time entertaining them. The Hayden children still adored Mary. At 11 A.M., Reverend Hayden arrived to pick up his children. At the sight of their father climbing from his horse-drawn carriage, the children screamed with delight, "Papa!" and made a beeline for their father. Tired and hot from his ride, Hayden asked Charles Stannard for a glass of water. Stannard took Hayden, who'd been his friend for years, into the house to give him a refreshment. Mary followed with the children.

As Hayden drank, he motioned to Mary to meet him by the spring at the edge of the yard. When he finished, he excused himself, and the pair sneaked off to the spring. Hayden told Mary that he'd purchased some "fast-acting medicine" to take care of the "problem." He asked her to meet him at the Big Rock after dinner, which they called their midday meal. It would be better if they did this alone, where he could take care of her if there were side effects from the medicine. Mary agreed, saying she'd use the pretext of picking berries to steal away from her family. They parted ways.

The Reverend Herbert H. Hayden did have a plan to solve the problem, though not the one he had outlined to Mary Stannard. For him, Mary Stannard herself was a problem that had to be solved—an expensive problem. Hayden had nowhere close to the $50 it would cost for an abortion. Moreover, he could not afford to allow an "easy" woman such as Mary to ruin his future as a minister by revealing her pregnancy—and its source—to the community. People who squealed like that were rats, and there was only one way to deal with a rat. Earlier that day, Hayden had traveled to Middletown and purchased an ounce of arsenic for a dime from Tyler's Drug Store. Arsenic in 1878 was sold legally in many drugstores and had many uses, including the killing of unwanted pests, such as rats.

Herbert Hayden knew that an ounce of the poison was far more than enough to kill Mary Stannard silently and cleanly. Hayden unwrapped the paper containing the arsenic and poured the contents into an empty pepper tin. He was careful not to touch the fine-grained powder. Then he changed into casual clothes and began to do some chores.

At about 2 P.M. he told Rosa that he was going to the woodlot to do some work. The area was swampy, so he said that he would travel on foot, rather than by carriage and horse. He left and slowly proceeded toward the woodlot. Once he was certain he was out of sight, Hayden altered his path, away from well-traveled roads. He must not allow anyone to see him, either with Mary or anywhere near the area of the Big Rock.

Finally, at about 2:30, he spotted Mary, sitting on a flat rock, looking pretty in her calico dress and sunbonnet. By her side lay a pail, ostensibly for berry collecting. Hayden saw the excitement on her face. Would it take long for the medicine to work?

Not long, Hayden told her. The reverend had little time to waste, and he did not wish to raise suspicion by being away from home for an extended period. In the pail, he put a small amount of water from a nearby spring. Mary then emptied the contents of the tin into the pail.

She drank. They waited. It was now about 2:45.

Minutes later, Mary's heart began to race. She bent over trying desperately to catch her breath. She jolted upright, clutching her stomach. Her breath was short and shallow. Her insides were on fire. Mary Stannard screamed in utter agony. She looked at Hayden, into his eyes. Had he . . . ?

Mary screamed again and began running in the direction of the Stannard home. Hayden, shocked that she was still alive after ingesting a toxic quantity of arsenic, raced after her. She must not scream; someone might hear her, and that could foil his plan. Hayden spotted a chunk of wood on the ground, and picking it up, he raised the block and slammed it into the right side of Mary's head. The blow opened a cut on her scalp, but it did not drop her.

Bleeding, wide-eyed, in agony, and moments from a death she now recognized as inevitable, Mary Stannard looked into the eyes of her lover-turned-assailant. She raised her arm to the gash on her scalp. As she did, Hayden struck her again, this time on the back of her hand. Mary finally sprawled to the ground.

Hayden knelt beside the bleeding girl; her breathing was faint. He withdrew his hunting knife from his pocket. Among his many skills, Reverend Hayden was also a former butcher. He repositioned himself behind Mary, to avoid the blood that was sure to spurt from the wound he was about to inflict. He lifted her head by her hair and untied her bonnet from her neck. Hayden jammed the point of the knife into the left side of her throat and drew the blade firmly across. He slashed her jugular vein, carotid artery, and larynx.

There was little blood; Mary's pulse was too weak to produce more than a trickle down her chin and neck.

Hayden rushed to the nearby stream and washed his knife and hands. He pocketed the knife. In one final attempt to make her death look like a suicide, Hayden laid Mary's body in supine position on the ground. He lifted her head and placed the bonnet beneath it, like a pillow. Yes, the people would believe that Mary Stannard had become so distraught that she had cut her own throat.

But there was one problem—a weapon. Clearly, Hayden could not leave behind his own knife. He could, however, return later with one of his son's knives and leave that as the weapon of suicide. But as it turned out, he did not have the opportunity to do so.

Hayden raced back home, making sure to cover his tracks as he walked. It was now 6 P.M.

The September 5 headline of the *New York Times* read: "A Young Woman's Ruin and Death. Mary Stannard's Dead Body Found at Durham, Conn.—The Manner of Her Death Unexplained." The reporter who penned the article took the usual journalistic license by opining that "the story of the clergyman looks like an invention and possibly was told by the deceased while in a distressed state of mind. It is said that insanity runs in the family."

Such blatant speculation was fueled when the postmortem on Mary Stannard revealed that she was not pregnant at the time of her death; subsequent examinations turned up a cyst on her ovary.

The results of the initial postmortem plus police investigation also made it clear that Mary Stannard had not killed herself, and Reverend Herbert H. Hayden was the prime suspect in her death. In the days following Mary's death and subsequent burial, the spotlight began to shine brighter and brighter on Hayden. The reverend was imprudent and impulsive, but he was not dumb; he soon concluded that the trail of rumors would lead police to him, and that he'd better come up with an alibi for the night of Mary Stannard's death.

The marriage of Herbert and Rosa Hayden was not one anchored in truth and honesty. The reverend's wife had long suspected her husband of philandering, and often at night her bed was cool beside her. But Rosa Hayden was a pragmatist; she knew her husband adored the children, and after all, what would she do without him? How would she survive if he were in jail?

She couldn't survive without him. So Rosa and her husband together concocted an alibi guaranteed to preserve his innocence and freedom.

Husband and wife rehearsed their strategy repeatedly until it became second nature—almost the truth. They considered every bit of evidence, every clue, every character strength and flaw in Hayden. They considered everything about the case except the one key piece of evidence of which only Herbert Hayden knew: the arsenic in the late Mary Stannard's stomach.

On Friday morning, September 6, the local sheriff arrested Reverend Herbert Hayden and transported him to Madison for trial. The communities of Rockland and Madison were abuzz with excitement as residents mustered to play armchair detective, and the local media—including the *New York Times*, located some one hundred miles southwest of these Connecticut coastline communities—readied pencils and pads for what surely would prove memorable fodder for news stories. Of all the pretrial madness, no story was more representative of the Victorian era than an article the *Times* ran on Edward Stannard, the grand juror (no relation to Charles Stannard and his family). Stannard had consulted a clairvoyant, who purported that Hayden had committed murder, according to anonymous spirits contacted. The paper ridiculed Edward Stannard and pondered why the clairvoyant had not spoken with Mary Stannard directly instead of anonymous spiritual sources.

Rumor and innuendo ran wild. One local man said that Mary Stannard had gotten what she deserved for blaspheming the reverend's good name. In Rockland, most of the townspeople judged

Hayden guilty. In Madison, where Hayden preached, most residents deemed him innocent. The battle lines were drawn.

Because Madison lacked an official courthouse, the trial of Herbert Hayden before the Justice Court was held in the basement of the First Congregational Church. Some five hundred curious folks jammed the hot, dark, and stuffy room on Tuesday, September 10. Henry B. Wilcox, the town's justice of the peace, presided over the trial. Wilcox had, only days earlier, signed Mary Stannard's death certificate. Like many others, he was deeply upset by Stannard's death and had battled a slight case of insomnia. Nevertheless, Wilcox refused to sign Hayden's arrest warrant, saying he'd prefer to sign his own death warrant.

Reporters from Connecticut and New York pushed and battled their way to get within earshot of testimony. Already, the Hartford papers had ranked the trial as one of the most noteworthy criminal events in the state's history. Again, yellow, tabloid-style journalism had prevailed over objectivity—at least for now.

The prosecuting attorney was forty-year-old H. Lynde Harrison, assisted by James I. Hayes and Edmund Zacher, both of New Haven. Hayden's team of counselors was led by Samuel F. Jones of Hartford, a top criminal defense attorney. He was joined by L. M. Hubbard of Wallingford and Tilton E. Doolittle of Madison. Because this trial functioned more like a preliminary hearing, there would be no jury.

As was often the case in the Victorian era, day one of the Herbert Hayden trial featured wildly contradictory testimony from "witnesses" who bent the truth to suit their own prejudices. The defense team scored well, however, when it brilliantly countered the testimony of Susan Hawley and Jane Studley. Judge Harrison ruled their testimony about Hayden's meeting with Mary, the alleged pregnancy, and even the letter written by Mary to Susan as inadmissible hearsay. In the Victorian era, hearsay constituted any "statement offered by someone other than the one who made it to prove the truth of the statement." The ruling was used to prevent a defendant from being convicted merely by a grudge held against him. Hearsay also came into play when the originator of the statement was unavailable. Mary Stannard not only was unavailable, she was dead.

Without secondhand information on which to base its case, the prosecution was in trouble. In trouble, yes, but not without recourse. Harrison ended the day's proceedings by adjourning the trial until Thursday in order to give the prosecution time to exhume the body and determine the type of medicine used in the alleged abortion.

Throughout the course of the first trial, the defense had attempted to turn the suspicion of guilt from Hayden to Susan Hawley and Ben Stevens. The media portrayed Charles Stannard as a farmer of the lowest class, which he was, and Stevens as another classless farmer who enjoyed his liquor—which he did, especially on the night before the murder. Stevens did himself little good by saying on the stand that he had never witnessed any signs of intimacy between Hayden and Mary Stannard. He also cast doubt on the charge that Mary Stannard had inherited some of her mother's alleged insanity; in fact, he defended the Stannards against such accusations.

The defense turned the naïve Susan Hawley into a defensive, moody, often hostile witness. She was, the defense claimed—and the media wrote—no better than the classless farmers with whom she lived or engaged.

Conversely, the defense's key witness, Rosa Hayden, became the linchpin to its case. Rosa played her role superbly. She elicited sympathy from the witnesses and audience by sitting in a rocking chair while on the stand to help ease her pain. She spoke with authority and conviction, yet in quiet, even tones. She presented her family as one that was happy, but not without the usual trials and tribulations encountered by any family. She confirmed most steadfastly her husband's loyalty and faithfulness to her and the children.

The details of her testimony further steeled her husband's defense: She had seen him go to the woodlot for wood. She had asked him to lend her his knife; Lennie, as Herbert Leonard was known, would use it to cut up some pumpkins and sticks. Lennie, the neighbors knew, was fond of knives and had two of his own. It was Rosa who had asked Hayden to go home on the night of the oyster festival to tuck in the children. He'd returned in just a matter of minutes, hardly enough time to seduce the Stannard girl, already known for her indiscretions.

Rosa Hayden not only defended her husband but also diverted the attention to another unlikely person: Edgar Studley. She claimed to have seen him on the day of the murder. Rosa also told the court that Mary feared that Studley would "force his attentions on her." It was an argument filled with bravado and hearsay, but one that Justice Wilcox allowed without question.

Herbert Hayden's testimony mirrored that of his wife, including the implication of Edgar Studley's involvement with Mary Stannard. Perhaps more important was the reverend's courtroom demeanor. He was the picture of self-confidence, convivial with witnesses and friends, often smoking cigars they provided. He came to court bearing a bouquet of flowers and a smile and hello for most everyone.

Judge Wilcox easily bought into the Haydens's stories. On September 25, the prosecution asked for a one-day continuance for their medical expert to complete the testing of Mary's organs for poison. Justice Wilcox, who had long since judged Hayden innocent, called the delay unfair to the defendant. The state then withdrew its case, unable to provide the data it needed to prove Hayden guilty.

Then Wilcox discharged Hayden on four primary points: the accounts of three witnesses that Hayden had not left the oyster supper for more than ten minutes; lack of evidence to prove that an intimate relationship between Hayden and Mary Stannard had existed; lack of evidence that Hayden acted guilty after the murder; and his belief in the truthfulness of Rosa Hayden's testimony.

Reverend H. Herbert Hayden was free—free to move his family to genial surroundings in Madison; free to return to preaching; free to forget about Mary Stannard. His freedom was short-lived, however.

By early autumn, the prosecution had compiled enough evidence to prove Hayden's guilt. The hub of their case surrounded the arsenic and the findings of Professors Samuel Johnson and Edward Dana of

Yale Medical College, two of world's foremost authorities on the poison. Dana had learned to identify specific batches of arsenic trioxide by examining the crystals under a microscope. His discovery was tantamount to determining the identity of an individual by his or her fingerprints. The professors' knowledge of the poison would launch forensic science into the stratosphere in the upcoming Great Case.

While everyone waited for the court terms to begin and end, Mary's body was exhumed three more times, its head cut off below the knife wound, and analyzed by Professor Johnson. The war between the arsenic experts and Hayden's church devotees had escalated, and rumor and speculation reached fever pitch.

In 1879, the case went to trial. The defense attempted to undermine the credibility of the state's witnesses. Susan Hawley and Ben Stevens—key witnesses for the prosecution—both came under attack from newly appointed chief defense counsel George H. Watrous. Susan was not as honest as she appeared, the defense argued. Susan, and not Mary, had written the letter to Reverend Hayden. Susan not only had helped Ben Stevens care for his mother, but she and Ben had enjoyed a healthy affair. When the defense asked Susan to provide a sample of her handwriting, she refused; like Mary and Charles Stannard, Susan Hawley was barely literate. Thus the defense, devoid of facts, used innuendo and fiction to move the emotions of the witnesses and jurors. Witnesses who were members of the church community even accused the prosecution of being "enemies of the church."

The entire tone of the trial changed when Professors Johnson and Dana and Dr. Moses White took the witness stand—and center stage in history—to testify that arsenic, administered by Hayden, had killed Mary Stannard. Before the jury of twelve, most simple local farmers, Dana embarked on tangential exposés on the workings of arsenic.

For three weeks, the courtroom became a scientific circus for the erudite. Dana testified that he could prove that the arsenic found in Mary's stomach was the same arsenic that Hayden had bought from the pharmacy in Middletown. He showed the wide-eyed spectators, jurors, and witnesses how he differentiated one batch of arsenic trioxide from another by examining the crystals under a microscope.

Numerous random crystals samples were brought into the courtroom, and Dana correctly identified each one. In fact, by studying and comparing samples from Mary's stomach and the tin, Dana demonstrated that the arsenic in her stomach was different from that in the empty tin, which had later been replaced by someone—perhaps Hayden. Two other professors provided additional evidence that arsenic existed in Mary Stannard's stomach, brain, and other organs.

Their reports and statements were brilliant—if one was a scientist. But to the generally uneducated jury and witnesses, the avalanche of specialized statistics, facts, charts, and experiments was overwhelming, numbing, and a means for the defense to negate the damning evidence and get Hayden off the hook.

Watrous was brilliant at confusing, tongue tying, and undermining the legitimacy of the professors and their evidence. For starters, the defense argued that such a large amount of arsenic as was found could not have remained in Mary's organs; it must have been placed there after her death. The professors had found twenty-three grains of arsenic, a staggering amount, in her liver, and it had even penetrated her lungs. The defense contended that such a large volume of arsenic could not have permeated Mary from stomach to brain in the few minutes she survived after drinking the poison. The professors debunked their argument by ingesting a small amount of arsenic. Within fifteen minutes, their urine showed traces of the poison.

Again Watrous rallied; surely the arsenic in her brain could have filtered there while she lay in the grave. The professors supported their evidence by running tests on other cadavers to show that this could not have occurred.

The more Watrous attacked the evidence, the more the experts corroborated their research and findings. Had this occurred in a contemporary trial, Hayden's fate likely would have been sealed. But forensic science was still in its infancy in the late nineteenth century, and jurors were apt to cast their vote based on other criteria—namely, prejudice and ignorance.

Watrous recognized this truth and redirected his attack to the professors' credibility and confidence in their findings. He attacked every statement uttered by the professors. Could they absolutely prove without doubt the accuracy of their findings? None of the professors could absolutely guarantee all of their findings. Eventually Professor White was driven to the point of exasperation by the defense counsel's constant needling, bullying, and grandstanding.

The upshot of this scientific bantering between experts and lawyers was a jury confused and unwilling to buy into the "claptrap" spewed by the learned professors.

What sealed the case for the defense, however, was the heartwrenching testimony of Rosa Hayden. As she had done in the judicial trial, Rosa put on a performance that reduced many in the courtroom to tears. Her performance, bolstered by the lies she and her husband had concocted before the first trial, made it seem clear that her husband was innocent of any wrongdoing.

In his closing arguments, Watrous compared Susan's "deceitful" face with the "truthful" face of Mrs. Hayden. He concluded by asking the jury for either a verdict of first-degree murder, which was more difficult to obtain than second degree murder, or an acquittal.

Of the twelve jurors who voted, eleven voted for acquittal. One juror, however, David B. Hotchkiss, held out for murder in the second degree. After fifteen ballots, Hotchkiss continued to hold out, angering the other jurors and rendering a mistrial. The state had the option to retry the case, but it had no money for a retrial and little hope of winning.

Reverend Herbert H. Hayden was free—free mainly because the jury had bought the story and respectable face of a "good" woman.

CHAPTER 3

A Cold Case Solved by DNA

✱ ✱ ✱

In 1973, the odds of a psychic contributing to the resolution of a murder were as unlikely as a human blueprint betraying the killer's identity. Yet both soothsayer and modern science helped solve one of the coldest crimes in Connecticut history—the July 16, 1973, murder of Concetta "Penney" Serra.

Serra's tragic tale began on a typically muggy New Haven morning. Serra, a twenty-one-year-old dental hygienist from New Haven, had taken a rare day off to pay some bills, run errands, and maybe even visit her boyfriend, Philip DeLieto, at the luncheonette where he worked. After winning a spirited tug-of-war with her sister Rosemary, Penney borrowed her father's car, a blue, two-door 1971 Buick Electra. Around 11 A.M., she drove off, headed for her father's auto garage downtown. Penney Serra not only was a gifted hygienist, but also did the bookkeeping for the family's auto repair business. After staying for about thirty minutes, she left to continue her errands. It was the last time a family member saw Penney Serra alive.

Where Serra went next is unclear. Earlier that morning, she had told her father, John, that she might stop at Malley's department store downtown and buy some furniture for the family. Such a visit would have led her downtown, through one of the state's busiest cities—called "Little New York" by some residents—to its new air-conditioned Chapel Square Mall, or to Macy's, the city's other large department store.

Whatever the case, garage and police records show that Penney Serra did enter the Frontage Road entrance of the Temple Street Garage, connected to the mall, at 12:42 P.M. She parked the Buick on the ninth of ten levels in the garage. One minute later, another car entered the garage, but from the George Street entrance.

What followed remains a mystery to this day. Serra may have been followed by the driver of the car that entered the garage one minute after her. The driver may have struck up a conversation with her, started an argument, and proceeded to initiate a chase throughout the middle and top floors of the garage, which ended shortly before 1 P.M. A few minutes later, an employee for the New Haven Parking Authority at the garage returned from his lunch break. After passing through the tenth level of the structure, he spotted a body at the base of the stairwell that led to the building's elevator shaft. The attendant walked to the corner stairwell and saw the body of a young woman lying in a fetal position on the bottom steps. She wore a light blue dress, which was covered in blood. Her arms and legs similarly bore streaks of blood, and her hands were dirty and caked with dried red-brown stains. She wore no shoes, and the soles of her feet, like the palms of her hands, were soiled. Investigators later revealed that her underpants and half slip contained traces of semen.

The surrounding lot was quiet, deserted save for a tan Jeep parked on the tenth level . . . and a brown wig lying conspicuously on the concrete of the ninth.

The garage employee observed these incongruities and called 911. Within two minutes, police cars arrived at the parking lot, and detectives rushed to protect the integrity of the evidence. Their investigation quickly led them to the lower levels of the garage. On the eighth level, in Section A, police found a blue 1971 Buick Electra 225. It was parked at an obtuse angle, as if the driver had been too harried to park properly. The doors were unlocked. Investigators searched the car's interior and were shocked at their findings: "reddish blood-like substances on the outside door handle and the door surface, on the steering shaft, on the floor of the driver's side, and on the aluminum trim both inside and outside the car." Police later theorized that the killer had driven the car from the ninth to the eighth level.

By 1:30 P.M., police had contacted the Department of Motor Vehicles and learned that John Serra of Huntington Avenue in New Haven was the owner of the blue Buick. Further inspection of the car produced a plethora of evidence, including a brown purse with the driver's license of Concetta Serra; a pair of eyeglasses; a Temple Street Garage parking ticket marked with 12:42 P.M. that day; reddish, bloodlike stains on the carpeting and in a tissue box; a colored mechanic's rag; and a white envelope smudged with the same reddish stains.

Although it was early in the investigation, police appeared to have ample evidence to track down Penney Serra's assailant. The investigation moved briskly when Nicholas Pastore, a chief inspector from the New Haven Police Department, took over the case. Pastore soon found a trail of drops and spatters of the same reddish substance in various parts of the garage, from levels ten through seven. At level seven, police discovered a set of car keys attached to a white key holder. They were covered in a sticky reddish substance. Nearby was a man's handkerchief, also spattered with a moist bloodlike substance.

Evidence technicians and detectives merged to sample the reddish, bloodlike substances, especially those found in and on the

Buick. The trail led from Serra's body on the tenth floor landing to the Buick, two levels below, and all the way to the fifth level. The same reddish bloodlike smears were discovered on the Jeep found on the tenth level, which police soon learned belonged to the New Haven Parking Authority.

Hopeful that the samples they had taken were from the blood of the perpetrator, police then dusted the Buick for fingerprints. They found several partial prints on the tissue box. Police also lifted prints from the interior of the car and the front ashtrays. They collected a number of cigarette butts and a store receipt, but with no store name on it.

Meanwhile, other investigators began to search for witnesses. A warm July afternoon in muggy Connecticut didn't provide for a busy shopping day. Still, based on the evidence at hand, police postulated that Penney Serra had run for her life, been overtaken by her assailant, and finally been killed. Surely someone must have seen or heard the struggle that ensued.

Early results were hardly encouraging. Chris Fagan, who worked at the ticket booth in the garage, recalled receiving a ticket, damp with what appeared to be blood, from one patron. The driver of the car was Caucasian, with long, dark hair. Fagan told authorities he had noticed that the man appeared to be injured on the left side and had asked if he could help. The man replied, "No, thanks," in a thick foreign accent. In leaving the garage, the man drove erratically, slamming over the adjoining sidewalk as he sped off. Fagan noticed the letters "AR" on the license plate. The car was a sedan of some sort, according to Fagan.

Another garage employee said he'd seen a woman running barefoot through levels five and six of the garage. She was being chased by a man who was thin, white, and had longish black hair.

A third witness, an employee at Malley's department store, also claimed to have seen a woman racing from a man on the eighth level. Her pursuer was a dark-haired man with a mustache. Unfortunately for police, this witness neglected to inform them that he had been smoking marijuana at the time of the murder.

By 4:30 P.M., the body of Penney Serra had been identified and transported to Yale–New Haven Hospital, a few blocks from the garage. An immediate autopsy revealed that a sharp instrument had entered Serra's chest wall between the fifth and sixth ribs and penetrated the right ventricle of her heart. Within ninety seconds of the assault, Penney Serra was dead.

Within hours of the murder, police had determined the cause of death, collected key bits of evidence, and found a few witnesses, albeit dubious ones. What they did not have yet was a motive for the crime.

They considered the most obvious motive: a relationship gone badly. Investigators quickly learned that Serra was romantically involved with a man named Phil DeLieto. In fact, the pair had recently called off their engagement. Still, according to friends of both Serra and DeLieto, the two maintained an intermittent romantic relationship.

Police obtained a warrant to search DeLieto's East Haven home. Their search produced a pair of scissors, one blade of which was broken and bore a reddish brown stain that later tested positive as human blood. Throughout the search, DeLieto cooperated with police; he even agreed to participate in an interview and police lineup. DeLieto emerged unscathed, boasting an airtight alibi for his whereabouts at the time of the crime—the luncheonette where he worked.

The next morning, local newspapers and televisions presented the shocking news of Serra's death, which, they noted, had occurred in broad daylight. Newspaper headlines touted DeLieto as the prime suspect. Such a pronouncement stunned the local community; Phil DeLieto was a distant cousin of Ben DeLieto, New Haven chief of police and the city's future mayor.

Newspaper articles trumpeted the off-again, on-again relationship between Serra and Phil DeLieto. Reporters scrutinized DeLieto's alibi: Yes, according to family members, he was at the restaurant all day. Numerous customers also corroborated DeLieto's presence at the restaurant during the time of the crime.

There seemed little question of his innocence—except that the community and media continued to keep the DeLieto name in the spotlight. Had the police chief provided special treatment to Phil? Was there a cover-up? That question would dog the DeLieto family for years to come. Rumor and speculation notwithstanding, detective Nicholas Pastore was running the investigation and calling the shots. Although he and Ben DeLieto often differed in philosophy and police matters, Pastore repeatedly lauded the police chief for his hands-off posture in the Serra case.

From a police standpoint, with Phil DeLieto scratched as the prime suspect, investigators had few substantive leads or a direction in the case. They did have a preponderance of questions, ones they would pose for decades. Top on their list: Why would anyone want Penney Serra dead? She was a typical product of the 1960s and 1970s—pretty, with long, brown hair and big, brown, imaginative and curious eyes that spoke to people. Serra loved rock and roll but valued her family even more. She worked hard and enjoyed hard work. She also enjoyed a comfortable life but was not overly materialistic. At the time of her death, Serra had fewer than $14 in her wallet. She also wore two gold chains, simple yet pretty. Neither had been broken during the tussle with her assailant.

This simple picture of Serra, wearing necklaces and with her money still in her purse, yielded one conclusion from the police: Robbery was not a motive. Serra's clothes also were intact, and other than the appearance of dried semen, there was no evidence of sexual assault. Her car, though parked at an odd angle, had not been stolen.

Could Penney Serra merely have been in the wrong place at the wrong time?

With forensic science in its infancy, police relied on their primary asset: manpower. Detective Pastore added four other experienced detectives to the case. Their first task was to identify the mechanic's rag recovered from the Buick. Their job was daunting; to find the owner of the rag, the team of detectives set out to visit every gas station and auto repair shop in New Haven County—twenty-five hundred businesses.

What they did not know, however, was that the mechanic who had left behind the towel, his partial fingerprint on the tissue box, and his knife in Penney Serra's chest worked nowhere near greater New Haven.

In October, the toxicology laboratory at the Hartford Health Department released its findings on blood samples taken from the crime scene. Bloodstains from the tenth level of the garage were Type A, the same as Penney Serra's. Other samples were Type O—the killer's?

Then there were the fingerprints: Prints taken from the Buick were compared with those of Serra and her family. Most of them were identifiable, except for the bloody prints on the tissue box. These did not belong to Serra, her family members, or even Phil DeLieto. They could belong to only one person—the killer. Still anonymous, still at large.

The Connecticut State Police Identification Unit began to compare the unidentified fingerprints against a state fingerprint databank. This system, rudimentary in design by today's standards, utilized a convoluted ten-point class system. To meticulously search the one million fingerprint cards indexed would have taken a technician from 1973 to 2025. Prints also went to the FBI's fingerprint identification division for analysis. None of them were identified.

As time passed and police were unable to turn up new leads, the local media began to tire of the unsolved case. Newspaper updates became less and less frequent, as reporters switched their beats to stories with substance. Increasingly frustrated with the lack of progress, John Serra began his own public-relations campaign to find his daughter's killer. He took out newspaper advertisements in an effort to find new witnesses. He wrote to the newspapers, talked with people on the street, and kept his daughter's death in his mind at all times. The community continued to whisper Phil DeLieto's name, certain that he and Ben DeLieto had orchestrated a cover-up of epic proportions.

After a year, the case had grown cold and had become a virtual nonstory to the media.

How desperate was the New Haven Police Department to find new leads? As the leads began to chill and wane, detective George Mazzacane consulted psychic and time walker Mary Pascarella Downey, who came up with the following clues: the color blue, the smell of garage oil, and water. Downey said that "blood would tell," and that it would take the police a "very long time to apprehend" Penney's killer. She also "saw" a uniform with a name tag bearing the letter "E" and "greasy hands being wiped on a dirty cloth." During the process, Downey developed a throbbing headache. At that time, no one knew how prescient Downey was.

Still, the case remained frozen until 1984, when a strange thing happened: a former classmate of Serra became the police department's first legitimate suspect.

Anthony Golino had been a star baseball player at Wilbur Cross High School in New Haven. In the late 1960s, he'd known Penney Serra, and locals suggested that the two had even dated. Golino was respected in his community, where he coached youth baseball and married his high school sweetheart in 1977. Golino may have thrown an unhittable fastball in high school, but he had no control over his tumultuous marriage. He and his wife had one son before divorcing—bitterly—in 1982.

The story could have ended there, had Mrs. Golino not contacted the police shortly after the dissolution of the couple's marriage. On July 6, 1984, the *New Haven Register* reported that Golino had told his wife, "I will do to you what I did to Penney Serra."

The comment aroused the curiosity of the New Haven Police Department. Police rounded up Golino and brought him in for questioning. Throughout the lengthy interview, Golino denied threatening his wife. Investigators asked how he had sustained the scar on his left hand—had it occurred during a scuffle with Penney Serra? Golino had no alibi. What blood type did he have? Type O, he believed, the same as the assailant's blood type sampled at the crime scene.

After the interview, investigators pursued a possible broken romance between Golino and Serra. One witness reported seeing them together at a local club; another remembered them arguing on a street corner.

The pieces of the puzzle were starting to come together. Golino's blood type matched that of the killer's. Witness accounts suggested that his and Serra's relationship was acrimonious, at least on occasion. Eleven summers after Penney's Serra's brutal murder, police believed they had found her killer in Anthony Golino.

Few in the community agreed, however. Many considered Golino the sacrificial lamb and Phil DeLieto the fugitive. By now, Ben DeLieto was the mayor of New Haven, and the police were ready to put away Anthony Golino for life. But the defense was not prepared to let this happen. It took the prosecution three years to prepare its case and overcome the numerous defense motions requested by Golino's attorneys.

Then this strange tale took another bizarre twist.

Some twenty-four hours before the start of the trial, a state-ordered blood test showed that Golino did not have Type O blood, the type believed to be that of the assailant. Charges were dropped. Additionally, Golino's prints did not match those dusted from the tissue box in the Buick. Most obvious, yet overlooked, was Golino's build: Weighing in at more than two hundred pounds and wearing a mustache, Golino bore little resemblance to the thin man witnesses claimed had chased Serra through the Temple Street Garage.

The investigation was back to square one. With pressure building—especially from John Serra—for the police to expand their investigation, John Kelly, chief state's attorney for Connecticut, took over the case. Kelly had the case reassigned to the Connecticut State Police Forensic Science Laboratory, headed by renowned forensic scientist and criminologist Dr. Henry Lee, and the State's Attorney's Office of New Haven, run by respected prosecutor Michael Dearington. Working together, this task force reviewed all of the witness statements and the evidence collected, and established a timeline for the murder. Lee found several inconsistencies between the witnesses' statements and the true order of progression of the crime.

It was by then 1988, and news of Penney Serra was about to explode across the country. Led by Lee and his team of forensic experts, the task force returned to the scene of the crime and conducted a crime scene reconstruction. Not only did the local media jump on the unusual demonstration, so did the national media. CBS sent reporter Mike Wallace to do a story on the Penney Serra case for its newsmagazine *60 Minutes*. In February, an estimated 20 million Americans witnessed the life and death of Penney Serra. Not surprisingly, CBS's producers went for the glossy story and fixated on Phil DeLieto and his relationship with both Ben DeLieto and Penney Serra. By now, Phil was happily married, and Ben was in the twilight of his political career. After serving in public office for years, he had finally gained the public's trust and admiration. Both were understandably disappointed at the focus of the segment.

With their roles now integral to the unraveling of the Serra case, members of the State Police Forensic Lab met on September 10, 1989, to conduct a reconstruction of the Serra killing. On hand were, among others, John Kelly and Michael Dearington. Based on witness statements, vehicular activity before and after the assault, time recorded on garage tickets, fingerprints, and photographs, forensic scientists determined a number of things:

The incident likely occurred on the seventh level of the garage and proceeded to the tenth level.

Either Penney Serra knew her assailant, and had a prearranged meeting with him, or the murder was purely random, likely the work of a psychotic.

Rape and robbery did not appear to be motives for the assault. Although traces of semen had been identified in Serra's undergarments at the crime scene, forensic specialists postulated that it had been deposited at another time. The origin of the semen's DNA could not be determined, and investigators believed the undergarments may have been washed subsequent to the introduction of the semen.

The blood trail started from the left side of the injured assailant and continued through the garage. It was vertical and snaked from level five to ten. The droplets likely came from a cut on the assailant's left hand.

All of the blood on and around the Buick was Type O, suggesting that it belonged to the assailant.

Only Type A blood—Serra's blood type—was found on level ten. This suggested that a struggle had ensued between Serra and her assailant. She fled from the ninth level to the tenth level, where the killer trapped Penney Serra at the base of the blind stairwell.

A single stab wound to the heart ended Serra's life.

At 1:01, the killer left the crime scene and ran to his own car, on the seventh level. En route, he dropped the blood-soaked keys and a white handkerchief on the garage floor. Next, he handed the blood-smeared ticket to the attendant, Chris Fagan. Then the killer drove wildly from the garage.

The reconstruction of the murder also included the brown wig discovered at the scene; early in the investigation, police had determined that the wig was incidental to the crime.

Four sets of fingerprints on and around the Buick, not visible to the naked eye, had required chemical and physical testing to make them visible. Under inspection, three of the prints were completely unidentifiable, and the fourth was little more than a bloody smear.

This crime scene reconstruction clarified what had likely occurred during the murder. Yet it still did not yield enough new data for police to determine the killer's identity. Forensic science was maturing, but Dr. Lee and the forensic laboratory still lacked the intricate computer imaging needed to reproduce the latent prints on a high-resolution monitor.

Weeks passed. Then months. Finally the 1980s came to a close.

In 1994, the State's Attorney's Office again thought they had found their killer. The suspect was not identified by name, described merely as an Albanian immigrant. Police had found his dental records in John Serra's car on the day of the murder. Serra later claimed that the records were not there when he lent his daughter the car. This suspect also had a long scar on his left hand. Two Superior Court judges refused to issue arrest warrants, however, citing inadequate evidence. Again the case went cold.

The evolution of forensic science, and the creation of the state's Cold Case Unit in 1998, not only helped identify Serra's killer, but also changed forever the manner in which investigators solved capital crimes. For years, Dr. Lee had lent his support to the case and, especially, John Serra. In 1999, Lee and the Cold Case Unit had the ability to identify an individual's identity through his or her DNA, the blueprint of life. The availability of DNA testing finally led police to Penney Serra's killer.

They needed a lucky break to get there, though. That stroke of good fortune came in 1994.

Edward Grant had spent most of his life working in his family's auto repair and towing business in Waterbury. In 1971, Grant was married and serving in the Connecticut National Guard. While on six months' active duty in South Carolina, Grant was seriously injured in a jeep accident. He sustained head injuries so serious that doctors were forced to insert a metal plate into his head. The operation probably saved Grant's life, but it came with a price: He suffered intermittent memory loss and severe mood swings.

After gaining his release from the service, Grant returned to Waterbury and the auto shop. In the late 1970s, he and his wife divorced, although he remained close to his family, especially his two children. By that time, Grant had earned a reputation in his family for violent outbursts. In 1994, his temper got the better of him. That summer, Grant allegedly beat his fiancée so badly that she had to be hospitalized. She reported the incident to local police, who arrested Grant and fingerprinted him. Although charges were later dropped, Grant's fingerprints had been automatically filed in the state Advanced Fingerprint Identification System (AFIS). In 1997, a Connecticut–Rhode Island fingerprint database recorded a match between Edward Grant's left thumbprint and the partial thumbprint left on the tissue box in Serra's car twenty-four years earlier.

The news of the hit energized the investigators and the investigation. They had a match for a person whose police record, demeanor, lifestyle, and profession fit the profile of Serra's murderer. Quickly, investigators contacted Grant. They advised him of his Miranda rights and the fingerprint match.

Police asked him how his fingerprints had appeared at the scene of the crime. Grant could not explain. They offered him an opportunity to clear his name by submitting to a blood test. Grant refused. Police next applied for and received a warrant to draw blood samples from Grant. They sent these samples to the forensic lab for DNA testing. The results were staggering: There was at least a 300 million to one probability that the Type O blood found at the crime scene belonged to Edward Grant.

In June 1999, detectives arrested Grant for the 1973 killing of Concetta "Penney" Serra. This was a bittersweet victory for the Serra family; John had died the previous November, eight months before Edward Grant's arrest. Rosemary Serra, Penney's little sister, was the sole surviving member of the family.

Still, there remained much work for the prosecution to complete. Defense counsel Thomas Ullman fought Grant's prosecution fiercely, arguing that the five-year statute of limitations had long since passed, thus rendering the arrest null and void. He contended that it would be unethical to prosecute Grant, as it had been nearly thirty years since Serra's death. Ullman expressed similar misgivings about the evidence, stored in laboratories in Meriden and Hartford since 1973. How could it have retained its integrity after all these years? Then there was the matter of the Albanian suspect never arrested despite being under police suspicion.

The prosecution team was equally skilled, however. Led by assistant state's attorney James G. Clark, prosecutors negated each of the defense motions. Clark emphasized that "long-established blood evidence practices, accepted by the courts in previous cases, as evidence that proper precautions and treatment had been taken."

In the summer of 2001, the prosecution emerged from this battle victorious. Scientific evidence would be permitted in the trial. On April 29, 2002, nearly three years after his arrest, fifty-nine-year-old Edward Grant appeared in Superior Court, to be tried for the murder of twenty-one-year-old Penney Serra. Presiding over the trial was Superior Court Judge Jon C. Blue. Blue was familiar with scientific evidence and the counsel for both sides. He had a reputation as a listener, one who was interested in the details of a case. That was good news for the prosecution.

The defense attempted to prove the existence of reasonable doubt based on Grant's alibi on the day of the crime and the shadow of doubt cast by the "at large Albanian suspect." The prosecution relied on the forensic evidence compiled by Dr. Lee and other forensic experts. During the second week of the trial, Dr. Carll Ladd, a lead criminologist in the DNA unit of the State Police Forensic Science Laboratory, questioned the state's 300 million to one ceiling that the blood sampled from the crime scene did not belong to Grant. The next day, Professor Kenneth K. Kidd, a Yale University geneticist, placed the DNA-matching figures at between 4.2 and 6.1 trillion to one that the blood samples were not Grant's. Of note, the forensic gurus explained to the jury that the genetic profile of one person could not change into another's, no matter the age of the sample.

The prosecution had the defense on the run. Dr. Lee's testimony further solidified their case against Grant. Lee used a scale model of the Temple Street Garage to punctuate his analysis of the assault and murder. He described how he thought the latent bloody fingerprints had gotten onto the tissue box found on the floor behind the driver's seat of the Buick. After running back to the lower level, the murderer got into the victim's car. He wanted to stanch the bleeding from a wound on his left hand, so he reached behind him as he started to drive the car through the garage. The tissue box must have been lying facedown, so the murderer had to reach around the car's bucket seat to flip the box over in order to extract tissues to stop the bleeding. In this motion, the assailant had left behind three bloody finger marks due to direct contact, none of which yielded any reliable ridges for fingerprint comparison. But in gripping the upright position of the tissue box, the killer left behind one clear fingerprint, his left thumbprint.

Grant, who had appeared confident at the outset of the trial, now looked shaken.

If Dr. Lee's testimony slammed the proverbial lid on Grant's coffin, Judge Blue hammered in the nails. He led the jury, seven marshals, a court stenographer, and the prosecution and defense teams on a tour of the Temple Street Garage and the scene of Penney Serra's 1973 murder. The demonstration concluded around 1 P.M., the approximate time of Serra's death nearly thirty years earlier. The tour was, as one *New Haven Register* reporter wrote, eerie.

Ullman fought valiantly for Grant, despite the evidence and the prosecution's momentum. But his case was significantly weakened when the prosecution disproved Grant's alibi. Yes, he had been in Vermont at the time floods swept through the area and precluded his departure. But the rain and subsequent flooding occurred in August 1973, not in mid-July, as Grant had claimed. With Grant's alibi negated, Ullman was running out of defense tactics.

He held out hope on one bit of evidence, seemingly discounted by the prosecution. This time, Ullman questioned the prosecution's failure to explain the source of the male DNA in the crotch area of Serra's undergarments. DNA tests had shown that the deposit of semen had broken down—possibly through previous washing of the clothes or, as the defense argued, through "environmental variables." Ullman hoped to show that if semen could break down over time, blood samples could be compromised as well, through improper storage. The defense furthered this line of questioning by summoning William Paetzold, an ex-employee of the Connecticut Forensic Sciences Laboratory, to testify. Paetzold testified that evidence from the Penney Serra case had been stored in a room that grew exceedingly hot—so warm that employees rushed to the room to warm up after being outside in the frigid New England winter. Clark rebounded during cross-examination by proving that Paetzold had neither experience with nor any knowledge of DNA evidence.

The defense then turned to Grant's ex-wife, who remembered him wearing dark blue pants and a work shirt to work, not green pants and a polo shirt, as witnesses alleged.

In the end, Ullman could have marched an endless line of defense witnesses to the stand; it would not have mattered. The forensic evidence spoke for itself. Grant's thumbprint and his singular genetic blueprint were at the scene of the crime.

On May 22, Judge Blue instructed his jury to begin deliberations. Six days later, fifty-six-year-old Edward Grant was found guilty of first-degree murder, nearly thirty years after the crime. In September, a judge sentenced the mechanic and Waterbury native to serve twenty years in prison. In April 2008, the Connecticut Supreme Court denied Grant's appeal for a new trial and upheld his 2002 conviction, thus officially closing the book on the thirty-five-year-old case.

Symbolically, however, the state had already written a fitting epitaph to Penney Serra's life and death.

On September 10, 2002, the state and town of New Haven had rededicated the new and improved Temple Street Parking Garage. Located at the hub of New Haven's downtown, the twelve-hundred-space garage had become a symbol of the city's efforts to resurrect its flagging economy. "If you don't have parking, nothing else works," Governor John G. Rowland said in the *New Haven Register*.

The ceremony did not mention Penney Serra's name, but those on hand could hardly miss the irony. Once an usher to the town's new Chapel Square Mall, trumpeting Macy's and Malley's department stores, the garage served as a painful reminder of what could have been: Not only did a vibrant young woman lose her life there, but in the years since Serra's death, both Malley's and Macy's had closed down. Enthusiasm for the mall and its stores had waned, and Penney Serra's death remained a specter over the city's failed economic plans. That reminder of death also descended over others involved in the case. In July 2008, Anthony Golino succumbed to cancer. He was 57.

So perhaps, with Serra's murder solved and a new parking garage augmented with electronic protection cameras and additional lighting, its rededication could have been called a rebirth of sorts.

CHAPTER 4
Forensics and a Brutal Murder

★ ★ ★

June 7, 2002: From her news desk at CNN, anchor Daryn Kagan studied the television monitor before her, waiting anxiously. Millions of viewers nationwide—especially those in Connecticut—did the same. All wanted to see Michael Skakel emerge from a Norwalk Superior Courtroom in handcuffs . . . and all hoped for a horrific chapter in the state's history come to a conclusion.

"He will leave in a prison or jail van, be taken to the Bridgeport Correctional Center, having been convicted in the murder of Martha Moxley," Kagan reported. "That verdict came down earlier today . . . to the surprise of many, including his defense attorney, Mickey Sherman, who says he will appeal that verdict."

Moments later, a shackled Skakel emerged from the courthouse and was escorted into a van that would take him to the Bridgeport facility. For nearly twenty-seven years, Skakel had enjoyed freedom and a privileged life, watching from afar as the family of Martha Moxley suffered with the memories of that horrific day in 1975 when then fifteen-year-old Michael Skakel brutally murdered their beautiful and effervescent fifteen-year-old daughter.

But now, only minutes after a Superior Court jury had found him guilty of first-degree murder, Skakel took his first steps as a prisoner, exiled from a privileged life to one of suffocating incarceration.

Many of the people on hand for the trial actually clapped in celebration of the verdict as the van pulled away. These same folks who had cheered Dorthy Moxley, Martha's mother, and her post-trial comments clapped derisively for Skakel as he was driven away. A covey of emotional onlookers began to chase the van, their cameras held aloft as they attempted to capture a picture of Connecticut's newest villain.

As Kagan and the stunned world assimilated the surreal scene, CNN correspondent Deborah Feyerick added her perspective. After pointing out that a very long time had passed since the tragedy had taken place twenty-seven years earlier, she said that she had spoken to one of Martha Moxley's friends who was in the courthouse. The friend had said, "You know, I sometimes don't know whether it helps or hurts Mrs. Moxley for me to be here," because, "I have a husband. I have children. I have everything that Martha never had a chance to have."

"A sad ending, you're right," Kagan concluded, "for two lives here, two lives affected at the age of fifteen back in 1975."

The ending, in fact, had taken twenty-seven years to reach. Tragic it was. But the beginning of the Martha Moxley–Michael Skakel story was anything but grim.

In 1975, Moxley and Skakel were teenage neighbors in the ritzy Belle Haven section of Greenwich, Connecticut. Greenwich was a wealthy and quiet town on the New York border, boasting mansions and private enclaves, expensive cars, excellent public schools, and privacy. Born in San Francisco, Martha Moxley had moved to Greenwich with her family in 1974. Moxley had little trouble fitting into this upscale community; a pretty blond with a broad smile, she easily made friends and became her high school class president. She made the boys swoon—especially the Skakel boys, Tom and Michael.

While Martha Moxley was popular in school and in her gated community, the Skakels were well known across the globe. The boys' father, Rushton Skakel Sr., was a brother of Ethel Kennedy, wife of the late senator and attorney general Robert Kennedy. He headed the family business, which manufactured carbon coke and was one of the richest family-owned companies in the United States. The Skakel–Kennedy tandem was one of the richest and most powerful families in the country—and a source of fodder for the press. Skakel was a business magnate, but he had struggled as patriarch of the Skakel clan after the death of his wife, Anne. Of the seven children, the boys, Michael, age fifteen in 1975, and Tom, age seventeen, spent many hours of their childhoods under the care of a domestic or their older sister or a tutor.

The Skakel boys found Martha Moxley to be a welcome addition to the neighborhood. Moxley, they soon learned, was outgoing and flirtatious, easy to like. So likable was she that the boys often fought over her.

On the night of October 30, 1975, Michael Skakel took the fight to a tragic end—only this time, the fight was with Martha Moxley.

Both the Moxley and Skakel homes were decorated for the Halloween season. And for Tom and Michael Skakel, Martha Moxley, and friends, the season began on Mischief Night, the precursor to Halloween, a usually benign—albeit annoying for adults—night of adolescent fun. Moxley, who had a 10 P.M. curfew, and her friends stopped by the Skakel home after their evening of pranks. Friends later reported that Moxley flirted with the Skakel boys and eventually kissed Tom. Moxley was last seen near the Skakels' backyard pool around 9:30.

That was the last time a friend or family member saw Moxley alive. When Martha missed her curfew, her mother, Dorthy, began to worry. As the minutes and hours passed, Dorthy became more concerned about her daughter's whereabouts—and, like many of the neighbors, nervous about the sounds that "went bump in the night."

At around 9:30 P.M. nine-year-old Stephen Skakel woke up to the sounds of an argument coming from the backyard. Despite hearing people scream, he fell back to sleep. Elsewhere, a twelve-year-old boy heard footsteps on the dense autumn leaves that blanketed the ground. He made a beeline for home. Another boy his age also thought he heard people screaming. A man let his springer spaniel out for a brief walk. Instead of returning home, the dog took off in a different direction. The owner beckoned the dog repeatedly. Nothing. The man went back inside his house. A short while later, he spotted the dog returning from the direction of the Moxley mansion. The man later reported that the dog seemed concerned and as though it needed to tell him something. A twelve-year-old girl in the neighborhood also heard a dog bark; the girl ran downstairs and then returned to her room.

Around 10 P.M., Dorthy Moxley heard what she later described as a commotion beneath her window. She noted what sounded like two or three men arguing. The Skakel maid also reported hearing a disturbance. Around half an hour later, a twenty-three-year-old neighbor suggested that the sounds were coming from the Moxleys' end of Walsh Lane.

And so on. Were these sounds attendant to Mischief Night pranks? Or did each of these witnesses get a glimpse of what was happening to Martha Moxley?

With her husband, David, out of state on a business trip, Dorthy spent much of a sleepless night contacting the neighbors in search of Martha. No one had seen her. As the night progressed into predawn of Halloween Day, Dorthy, neighbors and friends, and the Greenwich police kicked off a unified search for Martha. John Moxley, Martha's older brother, also conducted his own search, returning at 6 A.M.

without a hint of his sister's whereabouts. Exhausted, he neverthe-less dressed, ate, and went to school. Life had to go on.

At 10 A.M., Dorthy Moxley walked to the Skakel house, where she met an exhausted and frayed Michael Skakel. The boy had lit-tle substantive information to share with Mrs. Moxley.

Dorthy returned home and made two calls: first, to her husband, informing him of Martha's disappearance, and second, a follow-up to the Greenwich police, who had nothing new to report on the case.

By late morning, Sheila McGuire, one of Martha's closest friends, was worried sick by the girl's disappearance. McGuire also began to search the neighborhood. Finally, at about 12:15, the fifteen-year-old saw what she later described as a bundle resembling pink and blue camping gear in the Moxleys' backyard, under a pine tree. McGuire forced herself to walk over to it; finally, her eyes perceived what her mind could not conceive. The body of Martha Moxley lay facedown under the tree. Martha's pants and underpants were pulled down to her hips. Both scratches and deeper gouges ran from her hips down to her thighs. Her blond hair was almost entirely maroon with blood. The part of her face that was visible to McGuire was scratched and scraped. McGuire froze in her tracks. She was numb.

Somehow, an interminable few moments later, Sheila McGuire forced herself to walk to the Moxley home. She entered the house shakily and said she had found Martha. She could not bring herself to say that she thought her friend was dead. Dorthy remained stoic. A few minutes later, however, another friend of the family con-firmed the unthinkable: Martha Moxley was dead.

At 12:30, Greenwich police arrived on the scene. To be specific, two members of the department's juvenile division reported to the Moxley house. For two officers whose expertise was handling teenage crime, the sight of a dead young adult was as stunning as it was to the family. Greenwich had not investigated a murder in its own town in twenty-one years. The officers' immediate reaction was that a maniac had killed Moxley—maybe someone who'd jumped off the nearby Connecticut Turnpike bent on committing a robbery. That theory was short-lived, however.

From there, time and life became a blur for the Moxleys and the Belle Haven community. One of the Moxleys' neighbors contacted the family physician, who studied the body and noted that the beating to Moxley's head was so severe that the murder weapon had penetrated her skull. The physician even noticed bits of gray brain matter. He did not report the gruesome aspects of the murder to Dorthy Moxley, however.

Minutes later, David Moxley called from Atlanta; a neighbor who answered the phone urged him to get home. At first resisting David's persistent questioning, she finally disclosed his daughter's death.

Later that afternoon, John Moxley returned from school to find a neighbor awaiting him at the door, bearing the tragic news. Horrified, John responded with raw fury, throwing a punch at the man. Then he burst into the house, where he found his mother sitting in a near catatonic state.

In some ways, the Greenwich Police Department's response to the murder was just as shocking. Before long, the Moxley yard was teeming with uniformed and plainclothes officers searching for evidence. They were joined by neighbors and other curious onlookers. Unfortunately, in their collective search, police, friends, and family traversed the grounds that constituted the crime scene, including the lawn where the killer had dragged Moxley's body. This was just one of the missteps that would hamper the investigation.

Members of the local and national media descended on the scene, intrigued by the Skakel-Kennedy connection and fueled by the vested need to sell newspapers and dominate airtime with eye-catching headlines.

At 4:30 P.M., the Connecticut State Police Mobile Crime Scene Lab arrived and transported Martha's body to Greenwich Hospital. An hour later, police questioned Tom Skakel at length at the Greenwich Police Department.

Later that same day, investigators determined that Moxley had not died where she had been found. A trail of blood led from under the pine tree along a path to a pool of blood 150 feet closer to the Skakel residence. This blood was coagulating.

On November 1, Dr. Elliot Gross, the chief medical examiner, conducted a six-and-a-half-hour autopsy and determined that Martha Moxley had been killed with a golf club. Toxicology reports later indicated that Martha was not under the influence of drugs or alcohol when she died.

The next day, Greenwich detectives took as evidence a set of golf clubs that belonged to the Skakels. The clubs matched the description and manufacturer of the murder weapon. Not so fast, urged Rushton Skakel Sr.; the boys often left their clubs outside, and anyone could have picked up a club and used it to kill Martha Moxley.

Over the next six days, police administered two separate polygraph tests to Tom Skakel. The first was inconclusive—likely, police said, because Tom was exhausted. Skakel passed his second test; still, that hardly eliminated him as a suspect, for polygraph tests are not always reliable.

In between the two tests, Martha's body was laid to rest during a funeral attended by more than five hundred people, including curious spectators and the media.

While police interviewed a number of people, including the Skakel boys' newly hired tutor, Kenneth Littleton, Tom Skakel remained the subject of their focus. Based on witnesses' testimony, investigators determined several things about Martha Moxley's last few hours of life.

Tom Skakel appeared to have been the last person to see Martha Moxley alive. Michael Skakel, Martha, and two other girls had gotten into the Skakel's Lincoln between 9 and 9:30 P.M. Shortly afterward, Tom stopped by the car, ostensibly to collect music tapes, and climbed into the front seat next to Martha. Michael said that from his vantage point, he saw his older brother try a number of times to place his hand on Martha's thigh. She rejected his advances.

Minutes later, Michael Skakel left in the car with his cousins, but without his brother and Martha. Michael said he did not return home until around 11:30 P.M. Tom's story mirrored Michael's closely, although Tom contested Michael's statement that he had tried to touch Martha's thigh. He said that she and he had talked until around 9:30 (confirmed by at least one witness), and then she'd gone home. After that, he joined his new tutor, Ken Littleton, to watch a bit of the movie *The French Connection*. He finally retired to his bedroom to work on a paper on Abraham Lincoln, and went to bed around 11:30.

In time, the pool of suspects grew to three: Tom and Michael Skakel, and Ken Littleton. But investigators did not have adequate evidence to charge any one of them with Martha Moxley's murder. Over the next year, investigators dug deeper into the suspects' backgrounds.

Early in the investigation, the Skakels cooperated with police and were forthcoming with their memories of the night of the crime. Rushton Skakel allowed investigators to interview his sons at length. But when the investigation focused more and more on Tom, Rushton began to lose his patience.

Tommy Skakel already had a reputation as a hothead, especially at school, where his emotional explosions had become a source of conversation. Two incidents stood out: One time, Tom nearly strangled a classmate to death over a minor grievance. Another time, he tore a door off its hinges. In and of themselves, the two outbursts hardly qualified Tom Skakel as a killer. But within the context of the powerful Skakel-Kennedy family alliance, rumormongers kindled speculation of a cover-up.

On December 13, 1975, detectives interviewed Tom Skakel once again. This time, they also took hair samples from him. A month later, Rushton Skakel gave detectives written permission to obtain Tom's school, medical, and psychological records.

As pressure mounted on the Greenwich and state police to make an arrest, stress began to affect the Skakel family. On January 22, 1976, a beleaguered Rushton Skakel formally withdrew permission to release Tom's school records. Without these records, the investigation soon stalled. Later that same day, Rushton Skakel collapsed after suffering chest pains and was rushed to Greenwich Hospital. He then advised police that he had retained Manny Margolis as his son's criminal attorney.

For the next year, Tom Skakel remained the chief suspect in the murder case, as investigators strove to determine what made him tick. After initially refusing to take psychological and medical tests, as his attorney advised, Tom Skakel submitted to psychological tests on March 16 under a false name. On March 28, Rushton Skakel told the Moxleys that Tom had passed a psychological exam. He refused, on the advice of his counsel, to divulge the results of the test.

On April 30, Tom was admitted to Greenwich Hospital for further psychological testing. Two weeks later, the Skakels received a full psychological report on him. Tom's personal life continued to deteriorate over the next two years. In June 1978, he was expelled from college for poor academic performance.

While the police investigation turned Tom Skakel's life inside out, Ken Littleton, the boys' tutor, battled to avoid similar misfortunes. To police, Littleton was a curious suspect. Littleton had his own bad reputation and personal and professional baggage.

Littleton had been a star football player at Williams College but never made it to the NFL. Instead, he used his skills and experience in coaching. Two weeks after the murder, two Greenwich detectives paid Littleton a visit at Brunswick School, the private school where he taught and served as the football team's assistant coach. The detectives were surprised when Littleton vehemently refused to cooperate with their investigation. Was he just protecting Tom? Or was Littleton a bit unsettled psychologically? Their concern grew when a friend of the Moxleys reported that the tutor sunbathed in the nude in the Skakels' gazebo.

Such a lack of etiquette hardly made Littleton a killer. But over the next several months, Littleton failed a number of polygraph tests.

Further investigation into his background disclosed that Ken Littleton also had demons in his life. In the summer of 1976, he was arrested on Nantucket Island, Massachusetts, for burglary and felony theft. And there was more. A bouncer at one of the island's nightclubs, Littleton stood guard over the bar, dressed ostentatiously in a white suit with white shoes. He liked the way he looked, he liked the attention, he liked the girls, and he liked to drink. After hours, he often went to another bar, where he drank until he could barely walk. En route to his home, Littleton often stumbled onto homeowners' lawns and stole ornaments and other bric-a-brac. He then stashed the loot at home, like a pack rat, and occasionally sold the goods. One day, however, Littleton unwittingly picked a police informant as his target. Nantucket police intervened and uncovered $4,000 of stolen items in Littleton's home. He was arrested and charged with burglary and grand larceny. In May 1977, Littleton received five to seven years' suspended sentence for burglary charges in Nantucket.

Littleton not only had hot fingers, but also had a stubborn and noncompliant side. On February 9, 1976, detectives had returned to Brunswick School to get a written statement from Littleton. He was unavailable. In early April, Greenwich police once again attempted to interview Littleton. He refused. Two days later, Littleton again refused to speak with investigators; this time, he also declined to sign a statement about Tom Skakel. On April 13, Littleton retained a local attorney, and on April 22, he finally agreed to an interview—with his attorney present. Also in 1976, Rushton Skakel fired Littleton.

The tutor to whom Rushton Skakel had entrusted his boys' education and welfare had turned out to be a thief and a shady character. But investigators had nothing to show that Littleton was the killer of Martha Moxley.

Like his tutor and his brother, Michael Skakel also had his own proverbial skeletons in the closet. For the next few years, Michael's life spun in a downward spiral.

On March 5, 1978, Michael was arrested in Windham, New York, on charges of driving without a license, speeding, failure to comply with an officer (he was accused of trying to hit the police officer), and driving while under the influence. Rushton Skakel responded by sending his son to the Elan School, a private school in Poland Springs, Maine, that treated teens with substance abuse problems. Michael remained at the school for two years—in a manner of speaking. Twice in November 1978, he escaped from the school, only to be returned a few days later. On December 12, he again went AWOL. Perhaps most damaging were Michael's comments overheard by other students—statements revealed during his trial that ultimately sealed his fate.

While the well-publicized evidence hardly portrayed Littleton and the Skakel brothers as angels, it also didn't damn them to prison for killing Martha Moxley. Police continued to interview peripheral witnesses, and they lined up polygraph tests for Dorthy and John Moxley and John Skakel. Both the Johns passed their tests; Dorthy's results were inconclusive.

As time passed, the case grew colder, and investigators grew more desperate for answers. During the course of its investigation, the Greenwich Police Department sought assistance from both the Detroit and Nassau County, New York, police departments. They interviewed witnesses who had heard a dog barking on the night of Moxley's murder, and then followed up with Animal Control for complaints of a barking dog. Between October 30, 1976, and October 30, 1981, detectives conducted six overnight stakeouts of the murder scene—all on Mischief Night.

In 1977, David and Dorthy Moxley moved to New York City; son John did a year of high school postgraduate work at Choate-Rosemary Hall School in Wallingford, Connecticut.

On October 17, 1978, Governor Ella T. Grasso authorized a $20,000 reward for anyone with information that would lead to the capture of Martha Moxley's killer. Greenwich police twice met with psychics about the case. Despite their efforts to build a case around

Ken Littleton, investigators could not. The investigation and endless scrutiny took a toll on Littleton's mental state, however. During the next fourteen years, Littleton was treated for alcohol abuse and severe mental health problems. He moved to Canada, married, and eventually divorced.

The Martha Moxley case not only ruined Ken Littleton's career, but it also shattered David Moxley's life. A respected executive who worked long hours, he became the managing partner of a firm of noted Manhattan attorneys in 1986. Still, David found the time to pursue the investigation. The stress of running a high-pressure company and seeking closure regarding his daughter's death was too much, however. In November 1988, David Moxley died of a heart attack. He was fifty-seven years old.

The case could have died with David Moxley were it not for the efforts of three courageous individuals: Dorthy Moxley, Dr. Henry Lee, and reporter Ken Levitt.

A former investigative reporter for *Time* magazine, Levitt had covered the Moxley story on a national basis. At the height of his success, however, Levitt left the vaunted publication to freelance full-time. The Moxley investigation became his personal beat, and what Ken Levitt saw in the investigation bothered him. During a lengthy interview with Dorthy Moxley, Levitt learned that the state's medical examiner denied reporters access to the autopsy records. He then teamed with the *Greenwich Time* and sued for release of the records. Levitt and the newspaper won, but their victory was short-lived. The Greenwich Police Department went to court to obtain the right to edit—that is, censor—any story Levitt would write on the investigation. But the department lost the suit.

Still, when Levitt studied the police records on the case, he found little substantive information recorded. His conclusion: the Greenwich Police Department had badly fumbled the case. Levitt completed his investigation and then wrote a lengthy article on the case. Both the *Greenwich Time* and the *Stamford Advocate* refused to publish the story. Levitt's article, like the Moxley investigation, was stone cold.

Eight years later, both the investigation and Levitt's exposé came back to life. Ironically, it was a Kennedy who played a role in their revival.

In April 1991, rape charges were filed against William Kennedy Smith. Smith was a nephew of the late president John F. Kennedy and a cousin of the Skakels. Speculation surfaced that William Kennedy Smith had been at the Skakels' Greenwich home on the night of the murder. The rumor was later proved to be false, but it did rekindle interest in the Moxley case—especially in the media. As the local and national print and broadcast tabloids swooped on the Kennedy story, the Moxley-Skakel investigation regained some of the momentum previously robbed by community and media apathy.

On April 30, 1991, the Greenwich police and the state of Connecticut, with Frank Garr and Jack Solomon the vanguards, confirmed that they were reinvestigating the evidence. The *Greenwich Time* finally published Levitt's article, headlined "Moxley Murder Case Still Haunts Greenwich," on June 2. Then, on August 9, the Moxleys increased the reward to $50,000 and provided a toll-free number for people to phone in information pertinent to the case.

One of the resources the state used in reinvestigating the evidence was Dr. Henry Lee, the noted forensic criminologist and director of the Connecticut Forensic Science Laboratory in Meriden. For eighteen months, Dr. Lee analyzed both the forensic and investigative evidence and the available information on Martha Moxley's autopsy. He reviewed the information extant in the police reports. And as was his trademark, he reconstructed the crime and what had occurred at the crime scenes. In October 1993, he submitted a huge, six-inch-thick report on the Moxley murder. Lee's expertise in forensic science had helped determine the identity of the killers in other murder cases, but here he did not have ample evidence to finger Martha Moxley's murderer. Neither did the police.

Also that year, author Dominick Dunne, whose own daughter Dominique was murdered, published *A Season in Purgatory*, a fictional story with overtones of the Moxley murder. His book struck a nerve in the community; it would not be the last homage to Martha Moxley to do so.

In 1995, Levitt was back at it in an effort to break the Moxley-Skakel story wide open. Now a reporter for the Long Island newspaper *Newsday*, Levitt slammed the community with another eye-opening story on Tom Skakel. Levitt wrote that Tom had altered his original version of what had occurred on the night of Martha Moxley's murder. In the new version, Tom did not return home to do his homework as he had previously stated; now he said that he and Martha had had a prearranged date, one that began with "heavy adolescent petting" and ended with each achieving orgasm. Tom said that the rendezvous concluded around 9:50 P.M., when he returned home. Ironically, in 1976, Tom Skakel had passed a lie detector test in which he lied, saying he last saw Moxley alive at 9:30.

In early December, Levitt wrote a follow-up article on Michael Skakel. In the article, Michael also admitted having lied to police in previous interviews. Now he said that he and his older brothers had gone out that night to visit a cousin. He had returned around 11:30 P.M. and wandered into the night. His travels took him through the Belle Haven neighborhood, peering through the windows of homes. Finally, Michael reached the perimeter of the Moxley house. From there he climbed a tree and tossed pebbles in vain at what he believed was Martha's bedroom window. Having failed to rouse her, Michael then masturbated to orgasm.

The articles electrified the community and again kick-started the investigation. Providing some of the impetus was Dorthy Moxley. In the wake of her husband's death, Dorthy had become the family's vanguard in the investigation. On June 19, 1996, the Moxley family doubled the reward money to $100,000. Still, it took two more years for the next substantive movement on the case.

In 1998, former Los Angeles police detective Mark Fuhrman and his book, *Murder in Greenwich*, named Michael Skakel as the murderer. Fuhrman recounted the many mistakes made by the ill-equipped

Greenwich Police Department. Like Ken Levitt, Dominick Dunne, Mark Fuhrman, and Dorthy Moxley, Superior Court Judge George Thim decided to take the case into his own hands. He began an eighteen-month, one-man grand jury review of information gathered by Frank Garr and the State's Attorney's Office. Thim interviewed more than forty witnesses in secret sessions; soon word began to spread that Michael Skakel was the focus of the investigation.

Of note, despite the defense's failed attempt to quash testimony from patients at Elan School on grounds of doctor-patient confidentiality, two students provided testimony that was particularly damaging to Michael Skakel's defense. These students said they overheard Michael confess to the murder of Martha Moxley. They said he had bragged about killing Moxley with a golf club after she refused to have sex with him. He had also boasted that he'd get away with the murder because he was a Kennedy.

Despite his protestations, twice in 1999, a brittle Rushton Skakel testified in front of a Connecticut grand jury about the night of the murder. The last thing the seventy-five-year-old Skakel patriarch needed was more bad press for his sons. The negative ink had just begun to bury Michael Skakel, however.

In early December 1999, the grand jury completed its investigation, with Judge Thim finalizing his review on December 10. Thim now had sixty days to decide whether the evidence reviewed was enough to make an arrest. Still, even if Thim did determine that there was probable cause for an arrest, the prosecution was not forced to abide by his decision if it felt a conviction was unlikely.

At a January 19, 2000, news conference in Bridgeport, prosecutors announced that an arrest warrant had been issued for an unnamed juvenile. Defense attorney Mickey Sherman then told the press that Michael Skakel was about to surrender to authorities. At 3 P.M., he turned himself in to the Greenwich police, who charged him as a juvenile, as Michael had been fifteen at the time of the murder. After family members posted a $500,000 bond, Skakel was released.

By now the town and media were in frenzy over Michael Skakel's arrest. After twenty-five years, the horrific murder of Martha Moxley remained clear in people's minds—and newspaper pictures and blaring headlines enhanced these images yet further. Photos of Skakel being led away in handcuffs were displayed on newspaper front pages across the country. The broadcast media also trumpeted the story with shots of Skakel escorted by bodyguards and his attorney.

Next was Skakel's arraignment, the opening act of a media circus. In early March, Superior Court Judge Maureen Dennis ruled that members of the press would have access to the juvenile proceedings. She moved the arraignment to Stamford Superior Court, set for Tuesday, March 14.

Michael Skakel's appearance in court lasted a mere four minutes, but for Dorthy and John Moxley, it seemed an eternity. Skakel was advised of the charges against him and was read his constitutional rights. He was also notified of a reasonable cause hearing scheduled for June 20, 21, and 28, 2000. Shockingly, as Skakel left the courtroom, he stopped beside Dorthy and John Moxley and said, "I feel your pain. But you've got the wrong guy."

John Moxley glared back at Skakel and replied, "We'll find out in court."

The probable cause hearing garnered yet more headlines for the Kennedy-Skakel clan. Michael Skakel appeared in court supported by his brother, sister, and cousins Robert F. Kennedy Jr. and Douglas Kennedy. The highlight of the hearing came when witnesses from both sides testified as to whether Skakel had confessed to the murder during his stay at Elan School.

In August 2000, Judge Dennis decided that there was ample evidence for Michael Skakel to stand trial for the murder of Martha Moxley. But there was one problem: Attorney Mickey Sherman argued that Skakel should be prosecuted as a juvenile, since he was fifteen years old in 1975, when the murder occurred. But according to state law, a juvenile convicted of murder must serve four years in an "appropriate institution, one that would emphasize the defendant's rehabilitation." Skakel now was thirty-nine years old, however, and there was no appropriate juvenile facility for a middle-aged murder convict. In theory, even if convicted, Michael Skakel could be set free.

Despite the posturing of the defense team, Judge Dennis ruled in January 2001 that Michael Skakel should be tried as an adult. His probable cause hearing had shown that it was "well beyond mere suspicion" that Michael Skakel could have killed Martha Moxley. Sherman appealed the judge's decision, forcing legal motions to be resolved.

Finally, on May 7, 2002, the twenty-seven-year-old Martha Moxley murder case went to trial at Connecticut Superior Court in Norwalk. When Superior Court Judge John Kavanewsky banged his gavel to bring the courtroom to order, he signaled the beginning of a national event. The courtroom was packed, and dozens of curious spectators were turned away. Reporters for both print and broadcast outlets jealously reserved their spots behind the brick courthouse, their cameras, tape recorders, pencils, and pads at the ready. Inside the courtroom was a covey of writers, including Mark Fuhrman and Dominick Dunne. Media illustrators prepared their tools of the trade to record the emotions of antagonist and protagonists.

The debate over Michael Skakel's freedom began.

Sherman attempted to set the tone for his client's defense by comparing the many pieces of evidence to a jigsaw puzzle composed of pieces that did not fit. He characterized the prosecution's evidence as amounting to zilch.

In terms of forensic science, Sherman was probably on the mark. This was one of the few cases where Dr. Henry Lee's analysis of the evidence did not directly lead to the identity of the killer. There were many reasons for the paucity of viable forensic evidence linked to the body and crime scene. First, although investigators had attempted to cordon off the murder scene, numerous reporters, spectators, and

Elementary, My Dear Lee:
THE USE OF FORENSIC SCIENCE
TO SOLVE CRIMES

In today's technofuturistic world of crime solving, determining the identity of a killer has often become as uncomplicated as dusting for fingerprints. The use of forensics, the application of science to matters of law, gives criminologists and investigators the ability to see beyond killers' modi operandi and thumbprints and into their genetic blueprints. DNA analysis and index systems, image enhancement technologies, and automated fingerprint identification systems are just some of the tools forensic experts such as Dr. Henry C. Lee have used to crack cold cases.

Over the last twenty years, Lee pioneered the development and use of forensic technologies to crack seemingly unsolvable cases. Lee established the Connecticut State Police Forensic Science Laboratory and the Henry C. Lee Institute for Forensic Science at the University of New Haven and has lent his expertise not only to Connecticut's toughest cases, but also to some of the most notorious capital crime cases in the world. Locally, Lee contributed significantly to the solving of the Penney Serra and Martha Moxley murders. He garnered national attention for his use of forensics and his testimony in the Nicole Simpson and JonBenet Ramsey murders.

In many ways, Dr. Lee resembles Sherlock Holmes projected forward onto the starship *Enterprise*. Like all great detectives, Lee has an uncanny ability to spot significant crime scene details that other investigators overlook. Image enhancement technology helps Lee and other investigators visualize imprints and impressions, such as footprints or bite marks.

others trampled the path whence Martha Moxley's body was dragged. Key evidence was destroyed beneath people's footsteps. Second, because the medical examiner did not start the autopsy for approximately thirty-eight hours after Moxley's death, determining the precise time of death was impossible. Also startling to Dr. Lee was

Chemicals also enhance images and reveal trace elements, minerals, blood, and so on. Computers are used to enhance the images of videotape or photographs, often key to solving robberies.

Advances in computer technology have helped investigators track down drug dealers. Whereas in the past, police examined a murder victim's address book and bank records to seek leads, today they can obtain search warrants for the victim's computer. By searching the hard drive, police can track records of the victim's transactions and email chats. The data recovered can suggest a motive for the murder.

Still, these examples of forensic technology pale in comparison to the creation and development of DNA testing. Lee specifically used DNA analysis to solve the thirty-year-old Penney Serra case. Introduced in 1985, DNA analysis has been used in millions of cases worldwide and today is often used to solve cold cases. Whereas DNA analysis once took weeks and months to complete, it can now be done in just a few days. Most important, DNA analysis embraces many techniques, any of which may be used to identify the smallest bit of evidence. Other technological advances allow investigators to analyze even decomposed or degraded DNA samples. That means police now have the technology to solve a crime that occurred dozens of years in the past.

"DNA science has solved crimes considered otherwise unsolvable," says Dr. Lee. "In addition, DNA has ended the careers of serial rapists and serial killers, identified the remains of soldiers missing in action, established paternity in many instances, helped medical detectives to track diseases, and illuminated countless other controversies involving biological issues."

Were he investigating today, the great detective Sherlock Holmes might exclaim: "Elementary, my dear Lee, elementary."

the detectives' inability to locate bloody clothing in any residence in Belle Haven. Surely an assault of such brutality would have showered the perpetrator with blood.

Still, Dr. Lee's testimony was stunning in its power and description. Using charts and diagrams, Lee reconstructed for the jury the elements of the crime, beginning with how the killer first attacked Moxley from her left in the family's driveway. Moxley raced away, across the driveway and into the yard, pursued by her assailant. Here her attacker unleashed his fury upon her, smashing her skull repeatedly with a golf club. When little more than a sharp section of the shaft remained, he stabbed her savagely until the shaft went through the girl's neck, pulling with it her bloodied blond hair. Finally, the killer dragged Moxley's body another eighty feet to a spot under a pine tree.

Dr. H. Wayne Carver II, the current state's medical examiner, also testified. Although Lee and Carver acknowledged that they had found no physical evidence connecting Moxley to her killer, the prosecution had ample witnesses ready to shred Skakel's alibi.

Doubtless the testimony of the students at Elan School went some distance in planting seeds of a guilty verdict in the jurors' minds. Perhaps just as damaging was Michael Skakel's inability to get his alibi straight. A close friend of Julie Skakel's testified that she had seen Michael in his home shortly after 9:30 P.M. That directly refuted his contention that he was out, visiting a cousin, during the murder event.

The trial continued through May and ended shortly before Memorial Day. After deliberating for three days without a verdict, on June 7, 2002, the jury foreman declared Michael Skakel guilty of first-degree murder in the death of fifteen-year-old Martha Moxley.

Sentencing came on August 28 and 29, with the media crowding the Norwalk courthouse. Spectators queued at the front doors, and others hobnobbed with reporters behind the building. Finally the media and many of the onlookers rushed into the courtroom. The Moxley and Skakel families sat at opposite ends of the front row, with just a single spectator between them. When Michael Skakel entered the room, the Skakel family rose as one, in a show of solidarity. Dorthy Moxley, however, remained seated. She said softly, "I'm not standing for him."

Judge Kavanewsky heard witnesses from both sides. The following day, he rendered the sentence: twenty years to life in prison for the murder of Martha Moxley.

Reporters scrawled notes and cameras flashed, as the spectators stood wide-eyed. Finally Dorthy Moxley had found the closure that her husband, David, had not.

CHAPTER 5
Killing Spree

★ ★ ★

It is between 2 and 2:25 A.M. on May 13, 2005, at the Osborn Correctional Institution in Somers, Connecticut. Some three hundred curious people, many for and others against the death penalty, are outside the prison, awaiting the execution of arguably the state's most notorious serial killer, Michael Ross.

One proponent of the death penalty, Craig Miner, talks to a reporter. Miner points to the side of his car. On it is written "Ross must go, 5/13/05." He tells the Associated Press, "I have four kids of my own, and I really feel sorry for the families of the girls."

Others mutter about how Ross's execution could desensitize the state toward capital punishment and foster a wave of executions. Some stand still, looking blankly at the surreal scene.

Inside the facility, in a room with a view of the unthinkable, Debbie Dupris counts down the minutes until she will get closure on a nightmare that has run nightly for eighteen consecutive years. Dupris's sister was one of eight young women Ross confessed to killing in a three-year span in the 1980s.

The seconds tick away in this prelude to the first state execution since 1960—an execution of possibly the first person in Connecticut history to appeal in favor of his own death penalty.

Shortly before the half hour, Ross receives an injection that will grant him the peace he professed to desire after ending eight promising lives and shattering the lives of their friends and family.

Dupris watches intently as the man who kidnapped, raped, and murdered those women, including her sister, simply falls asleep. At 2:25 A.M., Michael Ross, age forty-five, is declared dead.

Minutes later, Dupris examines her feelings after witnessing Ross's execution: "I thought I would feel closure, but I felt anger just watching him lay there and sleep after what he did to those women. But I'm sure I will feel some closure soon."

It took Connecticut eighteen years to bring closure to a case that polarized the state over the morality of the death penalty and to end what became the soap opera life of Michael Ross. To understand why Ross not only killed, but also eventually sought equitable punishment for his crimes, it is necessary to review his life—unstable, to say the least.

For a middle-aged man who died in a state of confusion, Michael Ross came into an equally confused and tumultuous world on July 26, 1959. Whether Daniel and Pat Ross even wanted their son is a moot point; they did not marry until after Pat had discovered she was pregnant. A happy marriage it was not, even from the start. Daniel was a chicken farmer from Brooklyn, Connecticut, but Pat eschewed the rural life, which was anything but bucolic. In five years, Pat bore four children, underwent two abortions, and finally took off to North Carolina with another man more the vision of her childhood dreams. She did return to Connecticut but was institutionalized at Norwich Hospital, where, according to the admitting doctor, she babbled about suicide and hitting her children. Michael was her primary target.

The trial of Michael Ross revealed many gruesome details of his mother's abuse, including beatings and even an incident when Pat burned Michael's mattress after she caught him masturbating. Evidence also suggested that one of his uncles, who baby-sat him, sexually abused Michael, much the way Ross eventually did to his victims.

In later years, Ross said he remembered little about the negative aspects of his childhood. Most of the information on his youth is collected from interviews and court transcripts.

Somehow, despite the emotional and physical abuse he suffered, Michael claimed that he enjoyed his childhood on the farm. He especially relished helping his father, rising early every day and working hard, feeding the animals, and fixing the plows. There was, amid the tumult, a small measure of discipline. Still, for Michael Ross, it seems that even positive circumstances yielded the bizarre. After his uncle's death, the man's job of the killing of sick and malformed chicks with his bare hands fell to Michael, then eight years old. Ross killed them the same way he later killed his victims.

Ross had almost no memory of any problems in the family. To him it was a cherished farm life. "I liked the lifestyle," he said. "It's a hard life, but I think it taught me a lot of good things . . . Like you have to get up and feed the chickens every day. Just because you don't want to get up in the morning, you got to get up and do what has to be done. And if a piece of equipment is broke and it's 4 o'clock in the afternoon and it's quitting time and the chickens ain't been fed, that means you gonna miss your supper because you got to be sure the chickens get fed before you get fed. . . . I think a lot of kids today, I don't think they have the responsibility that I grew up with on the farm."

By the time Ross was in high school, his father relied on him heavily. "My dad knew that if he took a weekend off and was going somewhere, I would make sure that the eggs would be packed and the chickens would be fed, and everything would get done." Farm life imbued in Ross a sense not only of responsibility, but also of pride and passion. He loved the nose-to-the-grindstone work and learned everything he could about farming. In fact, from his early youth, Ross dreamed of becoming a farmer. He had the gifts to pursue almost any career; indeed, Michael Ross was tested to have a 120 IQ. After graduating from Killingly High School in 1977, Ross attended Cornell University and studied agricultural economics at the university's College of Agriculture and Life Sciences.

Like his father, Ross was a staunch conservative with simple middle-class values. He believed in the death penalty and eschewed the insanity defense, calling it a cop-out. Like farm life, his other future goals were idyllic as well: graduate from college, get married, return to his hometown of Brooklyn, and raise a family.

His freshman year was filled with promise. He had a girlfriend who was in the ROTC. He enjoyed his schoolwork. He was outgoing and social. He was a member of several organizations, including the Alpha Zeta fraternity and Future Farmers of America.

Then suddenly his life took a turn for the worse, with the circumstances mirroring those of his parents. The woman Ross was dating became pregnant and had an abortion. The news stunned Ross, who later admitted that he did little to support her financially or emotionally. When she later signed a four-year military commitment, Ross began a slow downward spiral. His simple dream of school, wife, and family had been shattered.

Now his demons had been set free.

Those emotional demons, ignited by an abusive childhood, slowly developed identities of their own. Ross began to entertain in his mind dark fantasies fueled by violent sexual images. During his sophomore year, he began to act upon those bizarre urges. Although he had fallen in love with a woman named Connie, Ross also began stalking other women on campus.

The fantasies became stronger, urging him to commit additional violent acts against women. Ross at first believed he could turn them off, much the same way an alcoholic claims he or she can stop drinking "cold turkey."

He could not. During his senior year, he committed his first rape. Later that year, he raped and killed another woman and threw her body into a gorge near the school. At this stage of Ross's twisted life, he was torn between doing wrong and right. At one point, he contemplated suicide by jumping off a cliff and into nearby Lake Cayuga. He lacked the guts to do so, however, and once again tried to convince himself never to harm another woman.

But he did, again and again. By 1984, Ross had killed eight women, ranging in age from fourteen to twenty-five: Dzung Ngoc Tu, twenty-five, a Cornell University student, killed May 12, 1981; Tammy Williams, seventeen, of Brooklyn, Connecticut, killed January 5, 1982; Paula Perrera, sixteen, of Wallkill, New York, killed in March 1982; Debra Smith Taylor, twenty-three, of Griswold, killed June 15, 1982; Robin Stavinksy, nineteen, of Norwich, killed in November 1983; April Brunias, fourteen, of Griswold, killed April 22, 1984; Leslie Shelley, fourteen, of Griswold, killed April 22, 1984; and Wendy Baribeault, seventeen, of Griswold, killed June 13, 1984.

Perhaps more mystifying than the crimes themselves was Ross's admission in interviews that he remembered little of the murders, merely bits and pieces of the crimes, all jumbled randomly. In fact, when interviewed by the police, Ross filled in the memory gaps with his own reconstructions, thus fictionalizing his crime-ridden autobiography.

By 1984, Michael Ross was an insurance salesman in Jewett City, Connecticut. Michael Malchik, meanwhile, was a police detective. In 1983, Malchik had been working on the stalled Tammy Williams case when he learned of the death of Debra Taylor that same year. Malchik studied the case notes and noted a similarity in the styles of the two crimes. Both women lived in the Danielson area, hardly a hub of violence, and both had similar builds. Other similarities prompted Malchik to conclude that the women were killed by the same person.

While Malchik was working on these two cases, Wendy Baribeault disappeared. Four days later, police found her murdered body, and Malchik was assigned to the case as chief investigator.

As everyone would discover, Michael Ross was a man with twisted, often arrogant views of himself and the world. As a killer, he operated with a sense of impregnability. It was this arrogance that eventually led to his capture. In the wake of Baribeault's death, several witnesses came forward and told police that on the day of the girl's disappearance, they had seen a man in a blue Toyota turn his car around in broad daylight and pursue Baribeault as she walked down the road.

Malchik ran a computer check on the car and found thirty-six hundred owners of blue Toyotas. He also had a description of the perpetrator. Although it did not exactly match Ross, who wore eyeglasses, Malchik had in mind one man. He made a beeline to Ross's home address. It was June 28, 1984.

What followed resembled a case from the Peter Falk detective show *Columbo*, where cop and perpetrator form an ironic bond to solve the case. Here Ross played the role of the brazen suspect, more than happy to lead Malchik down twisting paths in search of the killer. During their initial interview that day, Ross admitted to having twice been arrested for sexual offenses; this was information easily accessible to the detective, although it is unclear whether Malchik had done research to glean that data. At that point, Malchik decided to pursue the matter, demanding that Ross come to the police station and make a formal statement. Ross declined, preferring to report to the station after work, at 4 P.M. Malchik refused; he needed the statement now. (Malchick later denied saying this, however.) Ross later said that he had asked Malchik if he could call his father, but Malchik also refused this request, saying he could not until all of the confessions had been signed. Again, Malchik later denied saying this.

For the next four hours, murder suspect and detective played a circuitous cat-and-mouse game, culminating in their hypothesizing about the identity of the killer, particularly in the Baribeault crime.

When the interview moved to the police station, the pair talked as if they were law-school pals, aiding each other in the solution of a cryptic case. Ross later said that he believed Malchik was his friend, and the two of them were partnering to solve the crimes. Ross also later claimed that Malchik twisted certain facts to sound worse than they were "in order to prove extreme cruelty," a factor in his receiving the death sentence.

By the conclusion of their discussions, Ross had confessed to Malchik and the detective's partner of having kidnapped, raped, and murdered eight young women.

But *had* Ross confessed to committing the murders? In one of the many twists in this tangled tale, Ross admitted his guilt before the police read him his Miranda rights. Then again, was Ross actually in police custody during the interrogation at the station house? The defense later contended that once Ross had confessed to Baribeault's murder, he was in custody and had been seized without probable cause. Malchik argued that Ross was aware he was not being held against his will, nor had charges been filed.

Malchik's credibility came under fire in the coming months. So did the behavior of two Superior Court judges and a prosecuting attorney.

On November 15, 1985, Ross pleaded no contest to the murders of Tammy Williams and Debra Taylor. At his own request, he was sentenced to two consecutive life terms in prison—120 years in jail. But it was just the beginning of Michael Ross's slow walk to death row.

The trial, held in New London Superior Court, sparked a firestorm of publicity that swept over southeastern Connecticut. Ross's lawyers, fearing that the negative publicity and mood of the community would preclude their client from receiving a fair trial for the remaining six murders, conducted a public-opinion poll. Had locals already convicted Ross, in their minds, for the other murders? The results confirmed their fears, and a New London Superior Court judge concurred. The second trial, for the 1984 murders, was relocated to Bridgeport, some ninety miles west of New London. It is widely believed that this marked the first time a public-opinion poll and pretrial publicity necessitated a change of venue.

Two years after Ross's arrest, and one year before his second trial, his defense vied for the dismissal of two of the murders, those of Leslie Shelley and April Brunias, arguing that the two had not been murdered in Connecticut and thus were beyond the jurisdiction of the state. Their argument was moot; even if the women had been killed in a different state, the murders began and ended in Connecticut.

The state also brought to light a statement by Malchik claiming that Ross had provided him with directions to the crime scene. The detective stated that such directions were excluded from Ross's statements of two years earlier. Ross, moreover, denied ever having given Malchik such directions.

The defense attorneys added to the mystery by producing a piece of cloth that matched a slipcover in Ross's apartment. It was found in the woods of Exeter, Rhode Island, along with a ligature used to strangle one of the girls. They also brought to light a taped statement by Ross offering to take the police to the scene of the crime; Malchik later claimed he had no memory of such an offer.

During a closed hearing on the matter, Superior Court Judge Seymour Hendel exploded verbally at the prosecutor and police and announced that he had no doubt the murders had occurred in Rhode Island. Hendel questioned the veracity of Malchik's research and his honesty, but also praised the investigator for not wanting the other state to become involved in the case. When the court records were unsealed in 1989, Hendel retracted his criticism of the police officers, calling their findings a "judgment call at the time based on the information available to them."

As in most murder investigations, especially those with a death sentence on the line, "facts" change during the course of the investigation. In Michael Ross's mind, however, these discrepancies were the first seeds of discontent with not only the handling of his case, but also the trial that was soon to come.

The drama, the controversy, and the history-making trial began in June 1987, when Ross was tried for the murders of four eastern

Connecticut women. Ross was charged with the kidnapping, murder, and rape of Robin Stavinsky in 1983 and Wendy Baribeault in 1984. He also faced kidnapping and murder charges in the 1984 deaths of Leslie Shelley and April Brunias. Police found their strangled and beaten bodies in the woods of Preston, Connecticut, nearly two months after the girls' disappearance.

Ross faced the death penalty if convicted of any of the crimes. If so, he would become the first prisoner put to death in Connecticut since the state adopted a capital punishment law in 1980.

That Ross would make Connecticut history for such an ignominious note seemed likely; after all, he had already confessed to the murders of eight women, had already been convicted of two of the killings, and was scheduled to remain in prison for the rest of his life. What game plan, what ploy, could the defense employ to spare Ross's life?

The answer to that key question came via another question: Had the real Michael Ross snuffed out the lives of those young women? Or had he been driven by another voice inside his head, as he claimed during interviews? Through the testimony of psychiatric experts, the defense set out to show that Ross suffered from at least one mental or emotional illness, if not many.

At first glance, Michael Ross resembled anything but a killer. Bespectacled, shy, and introspective, he spoke at times articulately and intelligently. Other times he muttered simple, backward utterances characteristic of a farmer. He was the nondescript sort of fellow easily lost in a crowd. His behavior in Bridgeport Superior Court underscored that same sheepishness. During the four-month trial, Ross often seemed as if he wanted to hide. When he walked through the crowded hall of Bridgeport's Golden Hill courthouse, en route from the elevator to the courtroom, Ross refused to make eye contact with anyone, particularly the families of the deceased women. Each morning when he awoke, he memorized a script of what he would say in the courtroom. It was a script penned in the mind of a confessed killer.

The defense, led by counsel Peter Scillieri and M. Fred DeCaprio, relied on the testimony of psychiatric experts to show that Ross was clinically insane and had suffered from extreme emotional disturbance and an abusive childhood when he committed the murders. They had no illusion that the jury would acquit Ross, but by proving that mitigating circumstances had caused their client to commit the crimes, he would avoid a death sentence.

Scillieri, for one, knew he was facing a pit pull in New London state's attorney C. Robert Satti Sr. But no one could predict the controversial courtroom behavior—"blatant bias," as some witnesses told the press—of Judge G. Sarsfield Ford.

Afterward, Scillieri referred to the judge as unique, especially in his handling of the Ross trial. Fellow defense attorney DeCaprio believed that Ford was deeply offended by the nature of the crimes, as reflected in his courtroom demeanor and behavior. The *Day* of New London wrote that Ford opened his mail, clipped his nails, and acted bored or rolled his eyes during defense testimony. Ford's tone toward the defense counsel and psychiatric experts was viewed as demeaning and patronizing, according to reporters and a few of the expert witnesses.

To wit: the judge's handling of Tina Ross on June 17. Tina, Michael's sister, testified that her brother had grown up emotionally deprived and unloved. According to the statements of five witnesses, Ford then fired a stream of questions designed to unnerve her and undermine her credibility, including, "When you were growing up, did you have birthdays, did you celebrate Christmas, did you have exchange of gifts, were you in Girl Scouts, did you get awards, were you in school, were you in school plays, and did [your father] . . . provide an education for you and all the children?"

DeCaprio called Ford's verbal assault brutal. So did two of Ross's psychiatric witnesses, who felt that Ford's voice was too biased during the trial. Dr. Walter Borden, a New Britain psychiatrist who testified for Ross, said after the trial that Ford had whispered disparaging remarks to him while he was testifying. Other observers stated that they saw Ford roll his eyes and make facial expressions during Borden's testimony.

Dr. Fred Berlin, who also examined Ross, claimed that the doctors were not "heard very much" during the trial and were not treated respectfully. Later that month, Berlin filed a complaint with the Judicial Review Council; two years later, the council determined that there was insufficient evidence to "substantiate probable cause of misconduct." The complaint was dismissed.

State's attorney Satti also earned newspaper ink for his occasionally bombastic approach. For instance, near the end of the trial he dropped to his hands and knees to reenact particular moments in the murders for the jury. If Satti's aggressive approach shocked Ross, it merely caused DeCaprio to shrug. Satti defended both his actions and those of Ford in a statement to the *Law Journal*. He called criticism of Ford childish, saying it was "sour grapes and not deserving of direct response." Moreover, he said Ford's conduct during the trial was fair and impartial.

Not completely, however, as trial transcripts reveal. Just days before jury selection, Dr. Robert Miller, the state's psychiatric witness, wrote a confidential letter to Satti asking to be released from the case. Key to the letter was Miller's opinion that Ross suffered from a mental illness, sexual sadism. Miller, moreover, felt that there was mitigation to the murders, and that the death penalty was not merited.

During both the guilt and penalty phases of the trial, Ross's lawyers sought to introduce Miller's letter into evidence; both Satti and Ford refused. In 1994, when the case was appealed, the high court threw out six of Ross's death sentences because Judge Ford had refused to allow the Miller letter or report into evidence.

The courtroom theatrics of Ford and Satti did little to influence the decision of the jury, however. Satti's closing arguments during the penalty phase of the trial put the nails in Ross's coffin: "No way does the fact that a man is a sexual sadist say it's all right for him to go out and pick up any woman he wants, especially little girls, targets of opportunity, [pick] them up, rape them; and when you're done with it, kill them. No way, ladies and gentlemen, even if you find sexual sadism."

The jury agreed. After listening to three months of testimony, it needed just eighty-six minutes of deliberation to convict Ross of murder and four hours to choose his punishment—death.

The bizarre story of Michael Ross, confessed killer and now convicted murderer, could have ended with his death sentence. But the murders he committed and his history-making trial were mere preludes to the essence of Ross's story, which continued on death row and ended with a needle.

The tone and storylines of Ross's biography took yet another twist when doctors put him on antidepressants and antianxiety medications. One of the drugs, Depo-Lupron, helped quash the violent fantasies that had tortured Ross for years. While the medications virtually eliminated the production of testosterone, essentially castrating him, they also produced a heretofore not experienced sense of mental clarity. As a result, Ross began to examine his conscience, his actions, and his future—a future that, he eventually hoped, would provide the families of his victims with some semblance of retribution.

Michael Ross, who had used instruments to kill, now used another instrument—a pen—to speak out against capital punishment, question the judicial system, and reach out to the families of his victims. He did so in as many public arenas as possible and spoke his views to whoever would listen. While on death row, Ross also learned to be a Braille transcriber, and he promoted a support project that provided pen pals for hundreds of death-row inmates. Ross's PR campaign kept his pending death fresh in people's minds and the murders of their daughters in the minds of the families. Ross accepted the many interviews requested and spoke freely. It was a tactic that piqued many people, particularly Malchik, who questioned Ross's sincerity about giving back to the families from whom he taken lives.

As the weeks, months, and years passed since the murders, Michael Ross became a proactive advocate for his own death and the hub of a moral and psychological debate, at the center of which were Ross's mental competency and his right to choose his own death. In 1994, he wrote to several newspapers and to Satti, announcing his decision to forgo any further appeals. Then, because the trial court had rejected the admission of Miller's letter suggesting mitigating evidence that could lead to a life sentence, Ross won a new hearing from the Connecticut Supreme Court. But by the end of the year, Ross was in the midst of firing his attorneys while seeking to waive the new hearing. Why? In his letter to Satti, Ross said he was seeking peace of mind, and that the families did not deserve to suffer any more.

Ross was thirty-seven now and, according to witnesses and interviews, hardly the tormented person who had loved and maintained relationships with some women while killing others. Ross was personable, animated, and bent on finding closure for his wrongdoings. He'd taken responsibility for his crimes and admitted his guilt repeatedly. Yet he still sought to make it clear that mental illness was responsible for his killing spree.

"I am not an evil person, but merely a sick person," Ross said in an interview with the *Connecticut Law Tribune*. Scillieri concurred, calling Ross a "morally responsible person."

But Malchik disagreed vehemently. "He's hurting people terribly by doing this," he told the *Connecticut Law Tribune* in 1996. "I doubt the sincerity of what he's doing. How does a mother and father get over it? . . . Their life is over. He's destroyed their life. He's destroyed these people."

Malchik also suggested that Ross sought retribution for the families because he enjoyed the spotlight and desperately wanted to be known throughout history as the first Connecticut inmate put to death since 1960. Satti concurred with Malchik's belief that Ross, despite his purported good intentions, was merely restimulating the families' pain with his public remarks.

Dr. Walter Borden also bristled over Ross's desire to end his life: "He was obsessed with death, a kind of ultimate perversion, as a normal person would be obsessed with life . . . I think what he is involved in is nothing short of state-assisted suicide." Others felt that Ross's desire to die was little more than a symptom of being on death row for years.

Notwithstanding the many opinions of death penalty opponents, repeated appeals from friends and families, and professional evaluations of his mental welfare, Ross pressed on in his campaign for death. He hired T. R. Paulding as his private attorney to represent his case and, ultimately, help facilitate his death.

In 2005, Paulding explained his position to a national audience during an interview with CBS's Charlie Rose: "It's not something I ever envisioned doing. And I've said to my wife, 'If I do a good job, Michael Ross dies.'" Paulding's role was ironic as well. He was not only an opponent of the death penalty, but also a defense attorney. Was it not his job to try to spare Ross's life?

"That's an interesting thing when you put defense in front of the word 'attorney,'" he said. "I think I'm an attorney before I'm a defense attorney. Because, obviously, as a criminal defense lawyer, your usual role is either to have your client found not guilty or to arrive at the best result you can arrive at. But, I think your duty, your basic duty as an attorney, is to represent your client."

His client was competent, according to psychiatric evaluations. Even as the days left in Michael Ross's life began to dwindle to mere hours, Ross continued to fight for his death while others fought for his life and the state fought to revalidate his state of mind.

Meanwhile, Gerard Smyth, the chief public defender for the state of Connecticut, whose office had previously represented Ross, filed numerous unsuccessful motions up to the Connecticut Supreme Court, arguing that Ross was not competent, and that his office, not Paulding, should represent the man.

Ross even got support from unlikely sources. Vivian Dobson, whom Ross had raped in 1983, spoke out against the death penalty in the hopes of saving his life.

The battle over one man's life went down to the wire. In the predawn hours of January 29, 2005, when Ross was about one hour away from death, Paulding, acting on behalf of Ross's father, garnered a two-day stay of execution. Then, during the morning of January 31, Paulding got another stay of execution after reviewing new evidence that suggested Ross may not have been mentally competent. In question was new evidence brought forth in a book that Ross was pursuing his own execution because he suffered from a mental syndrome that affects inmates on death row. Was he really acting in the best interests of Ross? Paulding wondered. The attorney asked for, and got, another psychiatric hearing to determine Ross's competence. Ross previously had resisted numerous psychiatric evaluations, but he passed this evaluation from a court-appointed psychiatrist.

The dramatic story became even more suspenseful when the 2nd U.S. Circuit Court of Appeals in New York and the U.S. Supreme Court rejected last-minute appeals from Ross's relatives.

Michael Ross was about to get his wish: He would not grow old in prison, and the families of his victims could finally find closure. Ross had already found closure, it seemed. Toward the end of his tumultuous life, Ross became an oblate, an associate of the Benedictine Grange, a Roman Catholic monastic village in West Redding. In the hours before his death, Ross's family and lawyer visited him in his holding cell, near the death chamber at Osborne Correctional Institution in Somers. Ross brought with him a Bible, a book of Bible verses, a coffee cup, and some candy. His last meal consisted of turkey à la king with rice, mixed vegetables, bread, fruit, and a drink.

Of the three hundred or so people awaiting news of Ross's death outside the prison, not all were pro-capital punishment. "My heart is pounding," Suzanne Strum of Waterford told Fox News. "I can't believe Connecticut has become that state that's done it."

The tension outside the prison was palpable. Inside the death chamber, Ross appeared to be at peace. When asked if he would like to make a final statement before receiving the fatal injection, Ross said, "No, thank you." He shuddered once, gasped for air, and then became still, bringing closure to a life that had been filled with anything but peace. The time was 2:25 A.M.; the date, May 13, 2005. Michael Ross was forty-five years old. His execution was the first in New England since 1960, when Connecticut inmate Joseph Taborsky was put to death in the electric chair.

In the wake of the Ross execution, Dr. Stuart Grassian, a psychiatrist who had examined the convict and argued that he was not competent to waive an appeal, received a letter. It was from Michael Ross, dated May 10, 2005, three days before his execution.

The note read: "Check, and mate. You never had a chance!"

CHAPTER 6
The Wood Chipper Murder

* * *

"It is perhaps the most unusual criminal prosecution in Connecticut history. The conventional homicide has a corpse, so the fact of death is usually not an issue," said Walter D. Flanagan, state's attorney from Danbury, commenting on the "Wood Chipper Murder" in the May 15, 1988, edition of the *New York Times*.

When Joseph Hine punched in for his graveyard shift, snow and freezing rain had been battering Fairfield County for more than forty-eight hours. Frozen tree branches and power lines had snapped under the weight of ice and snow. The streets were caked with layers of snow, slush, and ice so thick that plows and sanders could do little to clean them. Hine, who worked for the Southbury Public Works Department, was one of the many employees vainly shoving his Department of Transportation plow along the local towns' main and side streets.

It was November 19, 1986, and Newtown, Connecticut, was in the midst of a fierce snowstorm. Hine had sanded and plowed more miles of caked-up roads than he could remember, but the snow on the streets this night showed no signs of melting. By 3:30 A.M., Hine had completed his work on the primary roads. Now he was navigating through the side roads, many of which were littered with and blocked by branches and tree limbs. He passed house after house, driveway after driveway, until . . . suddenly, the truck's headlights illuminated something out of the ordinary: a medium-sized U-Haul truck parked beside River Road, close to Lake Zoar. Attached to the truck was a massive commercial-grade wood chipper. Hine regarded the scene with mild interest, and then continued on his route when the driver of the truck waved him on.

Two hours later, Hine was on his return trip, plowing the opposite side of the road. The U-Haul had not moved; the rear gate of the truck was open, however. Hine squinted and made out wood chips scattered inside the truck and on the nearby road. He scratched his head. Who in the world would chip wood in the dead of the night, in the midst of a body-numbing snowstorm?

As it turned out, the owner of the wood chipper was a man who enjoyed toying with large machines. Richard Crafts, husband of Helle Crafts, father of three, and a resident of Newtown, a community of twenty thousand located in northern Fairfield County, did little to hide his passion for machinery. The family's front yard was strewn with landscaping tools, even a conspicuous backhoe that turned their property into an eyesore—at least to Helle and the neighbors. Crafts also enjoyed firearms. His collection included hundreds of handguns, shotguns, and grenades, and he frequently attended gun shows throughout the region.

Richard Crafts had been an Eastern Airlines pilot who made good money. He became a volunteer constable and by 1986 was a police officer in neighboring Brookfield. His fleet of "toys" included a Ford LTD Crown Victoria that he purchased, equipped with standard police radio, red and blue lights, and alternate-blinking headlights called "wig-wags." All were bought with money from the family's personal savings, leaving Helle to buy groceries and household goods with whatever remained from her paycheck as a stewardess with Pan American Airlines.

Crafts was blessed with an easy charm and sense of humor, which had attracted his stunning wife. The couple met through the airline industry. Raised in a small village in northern Denmark, Helle Crafts was pretty, outgoing, and smart. She spoke French and English fluently and could understand German, Norwegian, and Swedish. Helle made friends easily, and while living in France, she got her first stewardess job, with Capital Airways. She later moved on to Pan Am and met Richard Crafts in 1969. Crafts was not particularly good-looking, but Helle found his personality appealing. After dating for a time, the couple married in 1975, with Helle already expecting their first child.

Over time, however, Richard's hobbies and eccentricities unnerved the neighbors and slowly alienated Helle and eroded their marriage. But it wasn't just the toys that disturbed Helle; it was his distance and treatment of her that led her to fear for her life. She occasionally showed up at social functions bearing scratches and bruises on her face. Helle also told friends that Richard often left home for days at a time without telling her where he was going. With little money, as Richard constantly drained their budget to support his hobbies, Helle spent such days alone with little to do, wondering what her husband was doing . . . and what he might do to her.

By early 1986, Helle had told Richard and their friends that she wanted a divorce. She hired private detective Keith Mayo of Newtown to follow her husband and determine whether he was having an affair. Had it not been for the great blizzard late that year, Helle Crafts may have achieved her freedom. Instead, what happened to her shocked the community and nation, and advanced the use of forensic technology by light-years.

It all began—and ended—on November 19, 1986.

The snowstorm had killed the power in Newtown, and Helle planned to drive to the home of Richard's sister in nearby Westport.

The Craft children remained at their Newtown home; Richard called his sister and told her he would drive the entire family to Westport shortly. He did not show up until 7 P.M. Helle Crafts never showed up.

Charged with monitoring the activities of Richard Crafts, Keith Mayo had lost track of his own client. By December 1, Mayo had reached two conclusions: The disappearance of Helle Crafts was not of her own volition, and Richard Crafts had killed his wife. That day, Mayo called the Newtown Police Department, which reassured him that Helle had probably just left for a few days; perhaps she was having an affair and would return to reveal her secret.

Mayo thought otherwise. Helle Crafts was not the kind of woman to leave her family—at least not her children—even for a few hours. She was a devoted mother who funneled all of her love and passion toward her kids. She had little choice; as she had told her friends, she figured her husband was too busy sleeping with other women. Her friends looked at her bruises and at her husband's cache of firearms, and told her to get away—fast.

On December 2, Newtown police followed information provided by Mayo and decided to interview Richard Crafts. They thought little of Helle's disappearance. Richard had been a constable in Newton and was now a police officer in Brookfield; surely he had not done anything wrong. He claimed his wife had left on November 19, and he hadn't heard back from her. For the moment, the police adopted a wait-and-see attitude toward Helle's disappearance.

On December 4, Crafts took and passed a lie detector test. But although Crafts had put the local police at ease with his reassuring statement, he failed to convince the family's nanny, Dawn Marie Thomas. In fact, he changed his story to Thomas, telling her that Helle had flown to Denmark to visit her ailing mother. A family friend later debunked that statement by calling Helle's mother, who was in fine health. Helle's mother said she had not seen her daughter and did not expect to for at least a few months.

Thomas told police that on the morning of November 19, Richard had awakened her and the kids, had them dress, and then drove them to his sister's house in Westport. The nanny wondered why he would take them out in such dangerous weather, with visibility practically zero and the streets virtual ski runs. When they reached the Westport home, Richard quickly dropped off the children and left. He did not return until 7 P.M., without his wife.

Mayo took matters into his own hands. He contacted Walter D. Flanagan, the state's attorney from Danbury, and expressed his concerns. Flanagan notified the Major Crime Unit of the Connecticut State Police. The investigation into the disappearance of thirty-nine-year-old Helle Crafts had officially begun.

Step one was examining Richard's activities over the previous few months. State police quickly found credit card receipts showing that he had purchased new bedding and a large freezer, and had rented a piece of heavy machinery—the wood chipper—from a store in Darien. Their investigation of the Crafts home at 5 Newfield Lane in Newtown was just as alarming. After obtaining a search warrant, police officers, accompanied by biochemist and forensic expert Dr. Henry C. Lee, discovered a house seemingly hit by a tornado. The carpets had been torn up and removed; dirty clothes, mattresses, and rubbish were strewn around the house. The kitchen was equally unkempt, with dishes piled in the sink. Then there was the massive collection of munitions Crafts owned.

But there was no Helle Crafts. Then the investigation turned grisly, as Lee led a team of forensic experts in one of the most chilling and unusual investigations of its times.

Lee began at the Crafts home. He scrutinized every wall, floor, ceiling, and piece of furniture for traces of blood, but found nothing initially. Nevertheless, Dr. Lee suspected that there were traces of blood in the house somewhere that even the police had missed. As he worked his way through the bedrooms, the criminologist who had trained himself to see what others missed discovered on one mattress a few spots tiny enough to be overlooked during a typical investigation. He examined the stains with a magnifying glass, and then performed a presumptive test using an orthotolidine solution.

The test showed positive for blood, of the same type as that of Helle Crafts. Lee's investigation continued with the use of luminol and tetramethyl benzidine reagents on the bed sheets, towels, bathtub, and floors. Luminol was a brand new substance that glowed under ultraviolet light when in contact with blood. Even bedding that Crafts had washed repeatedly after the murder still tested positive for blood—blood that matched Helle's type.

Then Lee turned to the equipment. The wood chipper, called a Brush Bandit, was seized as evidence and disassembled. Lee's team conducted tests on the components but found no visible evidence of blood, tissue, or trace material. They did find evidence of hair and fabric fibers. Presumptive tests for blood were conducted in the machine's blade and bearing assemblies. The tests were positive for blood.

Still, because of the extensive cleaning Crafts had done not only on the house and furniture, but also on the saw and wood chipper, Lee did not have adequate samples on which to perform confirmatory testing.

At this stage of the investigation, Dr. Lee knew he was onto something, although it was circumstantial evidence he could not pin on Richard Crafts. Still, the picture was becoming clearer, and what Lee saw in his mind's eye was unthinkable: Richard Crafts had ground his wife's body in a wood chipper the way one would shred parts of trees into chips. Still, Lee needed physical evidence to confirm his theory.

Over a six-week period, detectives discovered an envelope addressed to Helle near the Housatonic River in neighboring Southbury. Also pulled from the riverbanks on December 30 were a chainsaw and serrated cutting board, with human hair and tissue in the teeth of the saw. As the snow melted over the coming month, detectives unearthed from the soil and chips 2,660 hairs, one fingernail, one toenail, two teeth, one tooth cap, and five droplets of blood. Then, on January 2, 1987, Dr. Lee examined the trunk of Crafts' Ford. Amid a scattering of wood chips were fragments of human flesh, bone fragments, and blue fibers.

Thanks to a variety of forensic sciences, state police believed they had enough evidence to put away Richard Crafts for life. From the evidence collected, police theorized the manner of Helle's death. Drops of blood in her bedroom indicated that she had been assaulted at the foot of her bed sometime on the morning of November 19. Police concluded that Richard next carried his wife's body to the basement, where the new freezer was stored. After placing her body in the freezer, Crafts returned upstairs to awaken Dawn Thomas, the nanny. He told her that because of the snow and massive power failure, he was taking the whole family to his sister's home in Westport. Crafts said Helle would meet them later in Westport. He drove them there, returned home, and then undertook step two of his nefarious plan. He took his wife's frozen body to a remote piece of property he owned in town. Police then believe he used the chainsaw to cut her body into smaller pieces. Crafts returned home and loaded the various body parts into the freezer.

The following day, when darkness had fallen on the town, Crafts wrapped the remains in plastic garbage bags. He proceeded to Lake Zoar, where he ran the remains through the powerful wood chipper. Crafts covered his tracks—or so he believed—by subsequently running pieces of wood through the chipper in order to purge the machine of any remnants of Helle's body.

Crafts, although deviously brilliant, did not realize that a few key pieces of his wife's bones, strands of hair, shattered teeth, and the letter did not make it into the water. He also neglected to consider that the town would be sanding and plowing the snow-caked roads, the reason town worker Joseph Hine observed the strange man parked by the lake with a wood chipper during a snowstorm. By this time, Richard Crafts had already completed his gruesome work.

On January 13, 1987, an arrest warrant was issued in Newtown Court for Richard Crafts. That night, around 9 P.M., a dozen Connecticut state troopers and detectives descended on the Crafts' ranch house at 5 Newfield Lane to arrest Richard Crafts. They ordered him out of the house. Crafts refused, saying he would "take care of it in the morning."

The police insisted he surrender immediately. Now piqued, Crafts ordered the officers to leave him alone. They continued to summon Crafts out of the house, beckoning him repeatedly by telephone. Crafts remained arrogantly defiant. Through the jousting, the Crafts children slept soundly in their beds. Finally, just after 12:30 A.M., a worn-out and distraught Crafts surrendered to police.

On January 14, the New York City tabloid the *Daily News* punctuated the circus atmosphere surrounding the investigation: "CHOPPED TO PIECES!" screamed the front page. Friends, family members, and, in fact, anyone who read that headline must have wondered what would have motivated the man to kill his wife in such a heinous way.

Those close to the Crafts knew that their marriage was a hellish travesty for Helle. Others—those curious or not intimate friends with the Crafts—would soon learn about Richard's secrets . . . and his evil side.

As the date of the first trial approached, and the bizarre story further circulated around the state and then the country, it became apparent that Richard Crafts would have a difficult time getting a fair trial in his hometown. The trial was moved across the state to New London, a hundred miles east of Newtown.

From the outset of the trial, the prosecution, led by state's attorney Walter Flanagan, used the research and testing done by Dr. Lee and his team of forensic experts and put many of them on the stand. Flanagan referenced the wealth of information gleaned from what appeared to the naked eye to be minuscule fragments. Dr. Lee stated that sixty-five pieces of bone were "cut with a heavy-type cutting edge that produced a crushing and cutting force." He added that the fragments of bone, hair, and tissue, mixed in with the wood chips, all came from the same machine.

Another key piece of evidence was the Stihl chainsaw recovered from the bottom of the Housatonic River during the search in late December 1986. Although the serial number had been filed off, technicians nevertheless had found fragments of human tissue, blond hair, and blue fibers that matched the rug in the Crafts home. The forensic lab in Meriden was able, however, to restore that serial number. Detectives traced the purchase of the saw to Richard Crafts on January 9, 1981, from a receipt Helle Crafts had turned over to private investigator Keith Mayo. It was one of many receipts she had turned over to Mayo when she'd initially hired him.

At this stage of the trial, the prosecution had proved that a human being had been mulched in the rented wood chipper. Now it had to prove that those tiny pieces of a destroyed life belonged to Helle Crafts.

The prosecution then turned to forensic odontologist Dr. Constantine P. Karazulas to prove that the remains were those of Mrs. Crafts. Karazulas testified that the tiny tooth fragment and attached piece of jawbone had been removed from the mouth with "traumatic force that sheared it off and took the bone with it." Had a dentist removed the tooth, Karazulas explained, the base of the tooth would have been clean and free of jawbone residue.

A second tooth sample yielded even more definitive evidence that it came from Helle Crafts. Dr. Karazulas testified that he had taken several hundred X rays of the recovered tooth, from as many different angles as possible. Karazulas then compared the X rays of the specimen against X rays of Helle Crafts's teeth, taken between 1980 and 1986. The recovered tooth at Lake Zoar was a perfect match to Helle's lower bicuspid in the X ray charts, according to Karazulas. Of this, he was "medically absolutely certain."

To steel its position, the prosecution called Dr. Lowell Levin, another odontologist, to the stand. Levin had made headlines by helping identify the remains of Nazi Dr. Joseph Mengele in 1985. A New York State Police forensic scientist, Levin also had confirmed for the U.S. Congress that the body buried at the John F.

Kennedy memorial in Arlington National Cemetery was indeed that of President Kennedy.

Levin took the stand and put an exclamation point on Karazulas's testimony: "That tooth, the lower left second bicuspid, belonged to Helle Crafts when she was alive."

The jury also had to consider the testimony of Rita Buonanno of Newton, a friend of Helle Crafts. Buonanno told of Helle's fear of her husband and recalled her saying, "If you ever hear that I've been in an accident or I'm missing, don't believe it."

The case went to jury on June 23. For seventeen days, the jury of nine men and two women debated for hours to try to reach a verdict. A trial already shocking in its content entered the absurd when juror Warren Maskell of Norwich held out for a not guilty verdict and refused to deliberate further and return to the courtroom. Judge Barry Schaller of Superior Court had little choice but to declare the epic trial a mistrial, doing so at 9:13 P.M. on July 15.

Afterward, frustrated fellow jurors said they had tried in vain to reason with Maskell but merely became exasperated in deliberations that were "hell," according to juror Janis Rosseau. During the trial, a hundred witnesses had testified and 650 exhibits had been displayed. All for naught.

Richard Crafts was free. Friends and family of the Crafts were stunned. So was Dr. Lee and his team of forensic experts, who had toiled around the clock for three months. All their work had been undone by one benighted and stubborn juror. The entire state buzzed over the outcome of the case, and newspaper headlines screamed louder and more sensationally than ever.

Still cocky, aloof, and defiant, Richard Crafts continued to plead his innocence in the days following the trial. But his freedom lasted a mere seven weeks. Because the first trial was declared a mistrial, the state could retry the defendant without a claim of double jeopardy. On September 7, 1989, the case went back to trial, this time in Norwalk.

Trial two was a virtual replay of its predecessor. Dr. Lee's evidence and testimony remained the cornerstone of the prosecution's case. The defense argued that none of the body parts could be conclusively identified as those of Helle Crafts. In fact, argued defense lawyer Gerard Smyth, the woman could still be alive. Richard Crafts was not only innocent, but also a victim of a conspiracy and sloppy police work. He argued that police had planted paper at the river and they had not adequately sealed off the crime scene. Without a body, they had proved nothing.

Throughout the testimony, the presentation of the damning evidence, and the debate between prosecution and defense, Richard Crafts remained cool and detached. He remained devoid of emotion when the trial went to jury on November 20. This time, the vote was unanimous. After a mere eight hours of deliberation, eleven men and one woman concurred: The evidence was in the chips. Richard Crafts was guilty of murder, nearly three years to the day after Helle had disappeared.

On January 9, 1990, Crafts appeared for sentencing. Again he pleaded his innocence and argued to Judge Martin Nigro of Superior Court that he was not the cold-blooded killer portrayed by the press. "I have feelings like everyone else," Crafts told the court.

Meanwhile, Karen Rodgers, Richard Crafts' sister who took custody of the three children, pleaded to Judge Nigro to impose the maximum sentence. "I am concerned that Mr. Crafts has not publicly nor privately demonstrated any remorse for the murder of his wife," said Rodgers. "I believe he has paid lip service only to the concerns of his family."

Judge Nigro denied the defense's motion for a new trial on the basis of inadequate evidence. He also said that telephone conversations recorded between Crafts and state police had been conducted legally. The defense contended that the avalanche of publicity against their client had prohibited Crafts from getting a fair trial. Judge Nigro rejected that contention as well.

On January 1990, fifty-one-year-old Crafts was sentenced to fifty years in a state penitentiary for killing his wife at home and feeding her body parts through a wood chipper on a bridge between Newtown and Southbury. It marked Connecticut's first murder conviction without a body and made the use of forensic science a key component in future investigations.

CHAPTER 7
An Ivy League Mystery

✷ ✷ ✷

On a chilly New Haven day in late November 2007, Ellen Jovin stood before a bank of media microphones and a team of reporters and pleaded for the police and the public to accomplish what local investigators had been unable to do for nearly a decade—find her sister's murderer.

Nearly nine years earlier, Jovin's sister Suzanne had been mortally stabbed seventeen times and left to die near the corner of East Rock and Edgehill Roads in New Haven. The death of the bright and talented twenty-one-year-old Yale University student stunned not only the entire Jovin family, but also the Yale community. Her murder spawned a controversial joint New Haven–Yale police investigation that shattered the life of a popular Yale professor, ignited a firestorm of protest and complaints in the community and media, and produced no arrests and no tangible leads in nine years. Details of the Jovin case were splashed across the pages of respected publications such as the *New York Times* and *Vanity Fair*; the ABC newsmagazine *20/20* also featured an in-depth exposé two years after the murder. The local media, in its haste to bring details to the public, turned the murder and subsequent investigation into a real-life soap opera.

Now, with many of the original investigators off the case, reassigned, or even deceased, a new investigative team, led by John Mannion, vowed to renew the stalled efforts to find Jovin's killer.

"This murder case is revigorated and renewed," said Mannion, former head of the state police Central Major Crime Unit, in an article in the *New Haven Register*. "We ask input from anybody who has information. Those who might have a repressed memory or something deep in their soul, please reach out to us."

Mannion's comments rang with irony. During the eight-year investigation, residents, members of the business community, and the local press had voiced their criticism of the way the New Haven and Yale police had handled the case. The sentiment: in their investigation, the police had merely reached toward one man, one named suspect snared in a web of circumstantial evidence.

That's what made the November 30 press conference outside of Superior Court in New Haven so intriguing. For the first time in nearly a decade since the killing, the local authorities were reaching in a different direction. Mannion confirmed that he would lead a four-member "dream team" of retired police officers in a new investigation. Mannion brought his twenty-one years' experience with the state police; Patrick Gaffney had served for fifteen years as a detective and sergeant in the Central Crimes Unit; Richard Wardell was a detective on the Eastern Major Crime Squad and Organized Crime Unit for twelve years; and Joseph Sudol's impressive résumé included time in the Central Major Crime Unit as a detective and command over the Computer Crimes and Electronic Evidence Unit at the Forensic Science Laboratory. To them, Assistant State's Attorney James Clark offered "full independence from all authorities." The team would reevaluate the information from previous investigations of the slaying while approaching the case as if it were brand new. Mannion added that no one and everyone was a suspect in the murder.

For the Jovin family, these assurances cast a sliver of light on a case suffused with darkness. For James Van de Velde, who had been emotionally treading water in a pool of distrust, innuendo, and suspicion since the murder, these were promises in the dark. Virtually from the beginning, New Haven and Yale University police had focused their investigation on Van de Velde, Jovin's senior thesis advisor and a popular lecturer at the Ivy League school. Operating with no tangible evidence against Van de Velde, police had not charged him with a single crime. Consequently, as the investigation entered its ninth year with little marked progress, one of the most perplexing capital crimes in Connecticut's history had morphed from a stagnant investigation to the story of a man ostracized and virtually ruined.

And so, with the case as cold as a New England winter, Ellen Jovin welcomed the renewed commitment of the New Haven Police Department (NHPD) to finding her sister's killer.

"We grieve for her every day," Ellen Jovin said of her sister. "If anyone out there knows what happened, please do not let one more day go by. Please call. Not knowing what happened" the night of December 4, 1998, "is devastating, and compounds the loss."

Ultimately, the Suzanne Jovin case is about people—two popular, brilliant, and immensely gifted individuals thrust into the public spotlight under the most tragic circumstances.

Until her death, Suzanne Jovin had enjoyed a fairy-tale life. A Yale senior pursuing a double major in political science and international studies, she was born in Gottingen, Germany, the daughter of American scientists Thomas and Donna Jovin. Suzanne was raised in a fourteenth-century castle and showed early in her childhood that she was immensely talented, both academically and creatively. By the time she enrolled at Yale, Jovin was fluent in four languages and had visited more countries than the typical ambassador. She was also prescient; some three years before the 9/11 attacks on the United States, she wrote her senior thesis on terrorist Osama bin Laden.

Immensely dedicated to her work, Suzanne Jovin also made the most of her limited leisure time. In high school, she sang with a number of rock bands and was equally adept at playing the piano and cello. She sang in both the Yale Freshman Chorus and the Bach Society Orchestra and cofounded the German Club. Jovin even worked for three years in the Davenport dining hall. At five feet, five inches and 125 pounds, Jovin also was athletic; she played squash, skied, and jogged.

In the days following her death, many friends referred to Jovin as a light of joy in her classes. Friends praised her sensitivity to social issues and her innate sense of justice. That sensitivity to others permeated her volunteer work, another cornerstone of her life. Jovin tutored urban children and was a devoted member of the Yale Chapter of Best Buddies, in which she and her classmates worked with and helped adults with mental disabilities. She hardly seemed the type of person anyone would want to murder.

If Suzanne Jovin's life story emerged from a fantasy book, Jim Van de Velde's came from a spy novel. At age thirty-eight, he was one of the university's most respected and sought-after lecturers. He possessed that unique ability to draw students into his political science lectures. In fact, *Spin* magazine rated his class called International Drug Trafficking: National Security Dimensions and Drug Control Strategies one of the most fascinating courses in the country.

His background was equally impressive. Hailing from Orange, Connecticut, Van de Velde graduated from Yale in 1982, followed by a doctorate in international security studies from Tufts University's Fletcher School of Law and Diplomacy. He went on to become dean of Yale's Saybrook College, where he oversaw the academic status of its 475 students. His reputation: conservative, proper, professional, and involved with the students. He also was firm, disciplined, and stuck to the rules—some students would say inflexible. His reputation was beyond reproach.

Van de Velde also held positions with the Pentagon and State Department, where he worked on U.S.–Soviet disarmament matters. He was trained in intelligence work as a lieutenant commander in the U.S. Naval Intelligence Reserves and enjoyed top-secret government security clearance. In deference to his top-secret intelligence work, the press often referred to him as cool or mysterious.

In the classroom, Van de Velde's "cool" demeanor transfixed many of his students . . . and ironically, it was these magnetic qualities that captured the attention of the police and media and kept Van de Velde in the crosshairs of the investigation. Van de Velde's larger-than-life image encouraged the police, media, and amateur sleuths alike to ponder whether this former altar boy who enjoyed a top-secret career, not unlike that of James Bond, could have killed one of his top protégés.

The attractive student and dashing professor first met when Jovin was accepted into Van de Velde's course Strategy and Policy in the Conduct of War in September 1998. Jovin was one of 40 students chosen from a pool of 160 applicants for that seminar and another of Van de Velde's courses, The Art of Diplomacy. From the outset, Van de Velde mesmerized Jovin with his realistic, hands-on depictions of the dynamics of international relations. He in turn enjoyed and acknowledged her enthusiasm for the seminars and passion for international studies. Jovin so enjoyed his classes that she chose him to mentor her on her two senior papers.

On December 4, 1998, both Jovin and Van de Velde spent time on campus doing schoolwork. Jovin wrapped up the second draft on her Bin Laden thesis. At around 4 P.M., she dropped off her paper at Van de Velde's office on Prospect Street. She included a note thanking him for his help and detailing the changes she had made to her draft. She suggested he contact her over the weekend to discuss the changes if necessary. She signed the handwritten note "Suzanne."

The weather was unseasonably warm that day—one of the tantalizing late-fall New England days that draws Mom, Dad, and the family Labrador out for a leisurely walk. Such was the case at Yale University's majestic, sprawling Ivy League campus, where the many neo-Gothic buildings magically blend in with a downtown busy with people of all types and countless bars, restaurants, and clubs. That night, students were out in number hustling from building to building, store to store, or simply tossing a Frisbee on a residential college quad. Others partied giddily, celebrating the conclusion of fall semester classes before their impending final exams.

It was a typically busy day for Suzanne Jovin. Shortly before 6 P.M., she walked to Trinity Lutheran Church on 292 Orange Street to coordinate a pizza-making party for her Best Buddies clients and their Yale counterparts. During the course of the evening, Jovin left the party to borrow a vehicle from the Yale carpool. She used the car to transport volunteers to and from the church. After the party had ended, around 8:30, Jovin dropped off one final volunteer and returned the vehicle to a parking lot on Edgewood Avenue, near Howe Street. She then walked the two blocks to her apartment on Park Street.

Before 9 P.M., at least two of Jovin's friends stopped by her apartment and invited her to see a movie with them. Jovin declined. She was tired and wanted to spend her night studying. At 9:02, however, she logged on to her Yale email account and, according to police investigations, informed a friend that she was leaving some books for the friend in the lobby of Jovin's building. Eight minutes later, Jovin logged off the computer and then left her building, clad in hiking boots, jeans, and a maroon fleece pullover.

She began to walk toward the Yale police office at Phelps Gate on College Street, between Elm and Chapel Streets, to return the keys of the borrowed car. Before reaching the police office, however, Jovin met up with classmate Peter Stein, also out for a walk. It was about 9:22 now. Stein later told the *Yale Daily News*, "She did not mention plans to go anywhere or do anything else afterward. She just said that she was very, very tired and that she was looking forward to getting a lot of sleep." According to the article, Stein also reported that Jovin was not carrying a backpack but did have in her right hand at least one sheaf of letter-size paper. The encounter lasted just a few minutes, and Stein said Jovin showed no signs of upset or distraction.

Then, according to witnesses and police statements, at about 9:25 P.M., Jovin left the Yale police grounds and headed north on College Street, toward Elm Street. She passed, without addressing, another Yale student returning from a hockey game at the university's Ingalls Rink. It was the last time Suzanne Jovin was seen alive.

At 9:55, police received a 911 call reporting a woman bleeding at the corner of Edgehill and East Rock Roads, in the well-lit, upscale East Rock section of New Haven. When police arrived at 9:58, they found Jovin lying in a pool of blood, facedown on the grass bordering the sidewalk and road. She had been stabbed seventeen times in the back of her head and neck. Her throat had been slit, and four to five inches of a nonserrated carbon steel blade protruded from her skull.

Jovin's clothes were not torn, however, and her earrings and watch appeared untouched. Police found a dollar bill in her pocket—they later recovered her wallet in her room. They also found, but did not disclose publicly for some time, a soda bottle in the brush near her body. Later tests revealed two sets of fingerprints on the Fresca bottle; one set was Jovin's, but the other prints have not been identified.

At 10:26 P.M., Jovin was officially pronounced dead at Yale–New Haven Hospital.

Within hours, news of the murder began to reach the quiet Yale campus. On the morning of December 5, students awoke to the shocking news of Jovin's death. Many students sobbed openly in the courtyard outside of Davenport, Jovin's residential college; others placed flowers by the gates of the building.

Later that morning, Van de Velde joined Yale's president, dean, chaplains, psychiatrist, and chief of police in a meeting with Jovin's college classmates. Van de Velde later that weekend appeared on a local television newscast, where he referred to Jovin as extraordinary.

On Monday, a visibly shaken and distraught Van de Velde returned to a numb class and placed a bouquet of three dozen white carnations at Jovin's seat. In an interview with the *New Haven Register*, he reiterated how remarkable Jovin was.

Yale University had not experienced a crime of this enormity since 1991, when Christian Prince, a sophomore and member of the lacrosse team, was shot to death outside the president's house. As with Jovin's death, Prince's murder stunned the campus; it also encouraged the university to invest an additional $2 million in campus security. (Yale has spent millions of dollars to protect its students on the many crime-ridden streets that surround the historic campus.) But Prince's death was different. Police had attributed it to a random shooting.

Within just a few days, investigators reached a conclusion that would take the case down a one-way street from which it would not emerge: Jovin's death was anything but random.

First, the murder occurred in a quiet, residential area of New Haven, about two miles from Phelps Gate, in a well-lit residential area. Police plotted Jovin's 1.8-mile route between Phelps Gate and the site of her murder. They determined that the only way she could have traveled the distance in twenty minutes was if she had been driven there. That the perpetrator did not take her earrings or money suggested that the killer was not motivated by money.

The lack of scrapes on Jovin's hands and the fact that her clothes were intact precluded a struggle. Based on the position of her body, police postulated that she had emerged from a car after talking—perhaps arguing—with someone she recognized or knew. There was no indication that Jovin had gotten out of the car and fled for her life.

Still, according to a police report, witnesses reported hearing "what sounded like an argument between a man and a woman." At least one witness reported hearing an argument and a voice crying, "Why are you doing this to me?" Others said they had heard a scream. Many witnesses reported seeing a tan or brown van parked near the site of the murder.

A New Haven police tip line report stated, "Police believe that someone she knew drove Suzanne there. It is very unlikely that she would have voluntarily gotten into a car with a stranger, or that she was forcibly abducted without someone witnessing something."

Following the available evidence and witnesses' statements, police focused their investigation on men Jovin had known. They interviewed and later cleared Jovin's mentoring buddy and her boyfriend, Roman Caudillo, who had taken a leave of absence after the murder.

On December 8, investigators visited Van de Velde at his home on St. Ronan Street and asked him to accompany them to the police station for a few follow-up questions. Van de Velde agreed to do so, without his lawyer present. Those "few questions" turned into a four-hour interrogation, during which Van de Velde calmly answered questions and defended his innocence.

Van de Velde shared some scant details of the interview with friends and his attorneys. The exact details of the lengthy one-on-one remain undisclosed, and the police have declined to release their version of the interview. According to Van de Velde, however, on the night of Jovin's murder, he had worked late at his office, reviewing Jovin's paper. He took a short break, walked to the rink to check out the Princeton–Yale hockey game, and returned to his office. He then went home and watched on television a taped episode of the comedy *Friends*. Then he ate a "month old burrito" and continued to watch television before retiring to bed.

Before leaving the police station, Van de Velde offered to take a lie detector test (he later passed one), give blood, and have his apartment searched. He even offered the keys to his red Jeep. Van de Velde emerged from the police station a free man; he had not been charged with any crime. He did not know, however, that for reasons unclear, the NHPD had made Jim Van de Velde their primary suspect in the killing of Suzanne Jovin.

The following day, Van de Velde was in his office when he read the following headline in the *New Haven Register*: "Yale Teacher Grilled in Killing." The story did not name the teacher, and the story was careful not to refer to the person as a professor. Still, it was not hard to figure out that the person in question was Van de Velde.

Shortly afterward, a numb Van de Velde emerged from his apartment and began to walk to a dentist appointment a few blocks away. En route, a television reporter and a cameraman stopped him. "Would you ever harm Suzanne Jovin?" the reporter asked on camera.

Van de Velde struggled to find the words. The image he presented on camera was of a man lost in confusion and despair. Stunned, he choked out a "no" and affirmed his innocence.

In less than a week, Jim Van de Velde had morphed from one of Yale's icons into possibly one of its greatest villains.

Notwithstanding the students' admiration for this larger-than-life teacher, neither the Jovins nor the police were ready to canonize Van de Velde. Van de Velde, police believed, was not always Mr. Prim and Proper with the ladies. The summer prior to Jovin's murder, Van de Velde had reestablished a relationship with a woman he'd dated previously. From there, the story gets nebulous. At some point, the relationship turned sour; the woman contacted the police and accused Van de Velde of harassing her, peering through her window, and stalking her. After Jovin's death, the local press reported that two women who worked for television had posted complaints with the police about Van de Velde's behavior. Both Van de Velde and his attorney Ira Grudberg scoffed at these reports, however, and Van de Velde was never questioned by police regarding these alleged incidents or arrested for them.

Students reported that Jovin had lost some of her spark for Van de Velde and his classes. She skipped two field trips that year and balked at a scheduled class project on terrorism. The assignment required students to research on the Internet how terrorists could retrieve information to build a weapon of mass destruction. When other students questioned the propriety of the project, Van de Velde canceled it.

Whatever conflict may have existed between advisor and student apparently peaked in the last days and hours of Jovin's life.

Jovin's friends recalled her being upset with Van de Velde over the way he handled her senior paper. Van de Velde had not returned Jovin's first draft of the thesis by the time she was handing in her second draft. In a March 2000 edition of the ABC newsmagazine *20/20*, a friend of Jovin's said she was "almost in a rage . . . Saying, 'I cannot believe this guy. I shouldn't have worked with him . . . Can you believe that he wouldn't even bother reading my essay until Wednesday?'" Jovin felt rebuffed by Van de Velde, even at one point brought to tears, according to her parents. Such an admission belied Van de Velde's usual supportive treatment of his students. Van de Velde typically returned students' emails within minutes of transmission; he even cooked "sesame noodles and Asian dumplings for students during a study break," one friend told *Vanity Fair*.

So why would Jovin think Van de Velde was avoiding her? He wasn't, according to attorney Ira Grudberg, who explained that the two simply could not find the right time to get together and discuss the paper. Van de Velde and Jovin did, however, review her paper on December 2, and Jovin seemed relieved, if not satisfied with their work, according to Grudberg.

"If she was reduced to tears, it tells me that she was overwrought with anxiety and wanting to do a great job," Van de Velde later said during the *20/20* broadcast. "And my name got caught up in the anxiety. But I don't understand how it translates into a motive for me to murder her."

Notwithstanding the conflicting evidence and information, police did see in Van de Velde adequate conflict with women to continue to investigate him. If he and Jovin had had a romance that soured, perhaps the rebuffed and outraged Van de Velde could have inflicted his revenge with a knife. Perhaps Jovin had rebuffed his romantic advances, igniting a suppressed rage that transformed him into a killer.

Perhaps . . . perhaps.

Perhaps, however, the local police had merely picked up the scent of an innocent man.

For weeks, a mutual *Yale Daily News* and New Haven Police Department investigation dug into the relationships Suzanne Jovin had shared with men, in particular Van de Velde. Their exhaustive investigation turned up no signs of impropriety between Jovin and Van de Velde, however. Moreover, none of the interviewed persons even claimed to have seen Jovin and Van de Velde together outside of office hours, and Van de Velde said he did not know where Jovin lived. He stated that he'd never had a relationship with a Yale undergraduate nor desired one. No one publicly disputed his claims. Yet local media and respected national publications such as the *New York Times* and the *Times* of London continued to fan the flames of speculation that Van de Velde and Jovin must have had an affair, using as proof the police's inability to charge Van de Velde with a crime or publicly eliminate him as their primary suspect.

Yale University also rode the anti-Van de Velde bandwagon when it canceled his spring 1999 classes, calling Van de Velde's presence on campus a major distraction. Quinnipiac University, where Van de Velde was taking courses, followed suit by dropping him from its master's program in broadcast journalism. Van de Velde later sued Quinnipiac for stating in the press that he had been removed from his position for "academic reasons." The university paid Van de Velde $80,000 in damages.

In January 1999, the NHPD officially listed Van de Velde as one person in a pool of five to ten suspects being investigated for Jovin's murder. That disclosure was superfluous, for the Yale and New Haven police, along with the media, had already made Van de Velde their proverbial sacrificial lamb. Still, the New Haven Police Department declined to charge this marked man with any crimes.

On May 6, the *New Haven Register* reported that Yale had terminated Van de Velde's contract; meanwhile, the university announced that the city of New Haven planned to award Jovin its Elm and Ivy Award for excellence in community service. In an ironic twist, the university pledged to recommend Van De Velde to other institutions, but with a caveat: He was under suspicion for murder.

The news, though not unexpected, raised eyebrows not only in the community, but also in the national legal world. Attorney and author Alan Dershowitz argued that Van de Velde's dismissal intimated that police had the power to influence the hiring and firing of faculty simply by fueling rumors and speculation. Dershowitz's show of support notwithstanding, Yale's decision to ax Van de Velde severed its relationship with a teacher who once had significant drawing power. Now the school considered him a pariah.

Still, administrators argued that the university was not attempting to distance itself from the case and its only named suspect. According to Ian Shapiro, chairman of the university's political science department, lecturers such as Van de Velde often stayed just one year because they fill posts left open by departing faculty members. Van de Velde was not even under consideration for an assistant professorship in international relations, his niche, Shapiro added.

When Van de Velde later sought several positions at Yale—assistant dean, assistant provost, residential college dean, and political science lecturer, his former job—Shapiro said the university did not have any openings for those posts; moreover, such positions typically were not awarded to one-year "visitors."

Van de Velde considered Shapiro's statements ironic, if not downright incongruous. Prior to Jovin's death, Van de Velde had been a huge asset to the university. His seminars were wildly popular, and students often were turned away from overbooked classes. Although university officials have never stated on the record that the Jovin case had a negative effect on the school and enrollment, their decision to cut ties with Van de Velde suggests that the school sought to look to the future. And Jim Van de Velde was a part of a painful past.

As the university closed this dark chapter in its vaunted history, the city provided the community and the Jovin family with a small piece of closure. On May 7, the city awarded Jovin and eleven other New Haven residents and students the prestigious Elm and Ivy Award. Yale president Richard Levin and Mayor John DeStefano Jr. both heralded Jovin's work with the Best Buddies organization.

Commencement Day 1999 was one of the most poignant graduation days in the school's history. On May 23, Yale University awarded Suzanne Jovin a posthumous bachelor's degree; she earned an A-minus in Van de Velde's class, and she graduated cum laude, earning distinctions in both majors. The emotional ceremony was an apt epilogue to Jovin's brief but unforgettable life story.

While Van de Velde's fight for freedom and honor was plastered across the front pages of newspapers and magazines, investigators worked surreptitiously, leaving the public with more questions than answers. NHPD Police Chief Melvin Wearing was especially tight-lipped. On the one-year anniversary of Jovin's death, he held a press conference that offered little new information. In 2000, Wearing declined to have a press conference at all.

Fifteen months after the murder, John Pleckaitis, then a sergeant at the NHPD, told *Hartford Courant* city editor Les Gura, "From a physical evidence point of view, we had nothing to tie him [Van de Velde] to the case."

Still, the police spotlight remained on its only reported suspect: Van de Velde.

With his career and personal life in tatters, James Van de Velde continued what would become an ongoing quest for freedom and redemption. The Jovin family, similarly, refused to allow the investigation to halt. By using the national broadcast and print media, both the chief suspect and the victim's family pressured the police to reexamine the modus operandi of their investigation.

The newsmagazine *20/20* was hardly complimentary of the investigation, and reporter John Miller repeatedly took the NHPD as well as Yale University, officials from which declined to be interviewed for the program, to task. For instance, the program disclosed a quote from a university spokesman alleging that Yale wanted to "move on, that attention to the murder 'can only hurt Yale.'" The network later identified Thomas Conroy, Yale's deputy director of public affairs at the time of the program, as the source of the quote.

Conroy subsequently denied making the statements; Linda Lorimer, vice president and university secretary, also refuted the statement in a release.

Miller discussed the case with Dr. Henry Lee, the criminologist and forensic specialist. Dr. Lee said that the police did allow him to examine the clothing that Jovin had been wearing when she was murdered. Still, he told Miller that he had offered to visit the crime scene the night Jovin was murdered, but the police turned him down.

On March 30, 2000, the *Yale Daily News* published a letter from Jovin's parents in response to the *20/20* broadcast and the university's reaction. "The statements by the Yale College administration in reaction to the outcry on and off campus to the callous position of the University reported in the '20/20' program are disingenuous, hypocritical [and] self-serving," they wrote. "It was a tragic mistake to send our daughter to Yale."

Van de Velde commented, "I have no doubt, therefore, that [Yale president Richard] Levin and Lorimer specifically wrote or approved the Yale statement."

In late 2000, the Jovins pressured Yale into hiring two retired policemen to undertake a private investigation of the crime. The university also posted a $100,000 reward, to augment the $50,000 reward previously offered by the state, for information leading to the arrest of the Suzanne Jovin's killer.

Was this the break the Jovins and Van de Velde needed?

The investigating team of Andrew Rosenzweig and Patrick Harnett boasted years of experience in handling cold cases. Rosenzweig was the chief investigator for the Manhattan District Attorney's Office, and he had made headlines by solving a double homicide after thirty years had passed. Harnett was a longtime NYPD officer who had worked on the "Son of Sam" case and numerous investigations of organized crime. His success in the field earned him a promotion to commanding officer of the major crime squad.

For more than six months, Rosenzweig and Harnett investigated the Jovin case meticulously. Their efforts produced little substantive evidence, yet they did persuade the New Haven police to allow the state forensic lab to analyze Jovin's fingernail scrapings for DNA. They found that neither the DNA taken nor the fingerprints on the Fresca bottle matched those of Van de Velde.

The investigation was back to square one, and Van de Velde remained on the interminable emotional roller coaster ride. In 2001, he sued the *Hartford Courant* for running a story that said he had "inappropriately visited the home of a woman he dated in 1997." The paper corrected the story and, shortly after, published an article that painted a different picture of the case.

In the April 1, 2001, edition of the *Courant*, city editor Les Gura asked his readers, "Are You Wrong about James Van de Velde?" The article sympathized with Van de Velde and his plight, being the sole, though noncharged, publicly named suspect. The article criticized the manner in which the police, Yale, and the media had handled the case. Ultimately, Gura questioned the logic of even considering Van de Velde a suspect. How could this suspected killer ever prove his innocence when, on the night of the murder, he was alone in his apartment watching television? Gura punctuated the theme of the story when he called Van de Velde's mission to prove his innocence "all but impossible."

Van de Velde received his second potential big break that October, when the headline "Test Shows DNA Not from Jovin's Yale Advisor" flashed across local newspapers and television screens. The announcement came nearly three years after the murder had been committed. The DNA samples also did not match those taken from Jovin's boyfriend and numerous emergency personnel at the murder scene. Investigators now would seek samples from Jovin's friends.

Almost as intriguing was the manner in which the reticent police department disclosed the information. Rather than announce the findings publicly in a press conference, and thus be forced to answer questions regarding the case, New Haven area state's attorney Michael Dearington released the information in a written announcement distributed to media outlets. The release contained no public apology to Van de Velde, who was in the Middle East on a U.S. government intelligence mission and operating with high security clearance at the time of the announcement.

Frustrated by the police department's refusal to officially eliminate him as a suspect, Van de Velde became his own public-relations machine, using the media, websites, and blogs in an attempt to prove his innocence. He was not alone in this effort to clear his name and energize the investigation, however. In 1999, Van de Velde's close friend Jeffrey Mitchell opened an Internet message board dedicated to solving the murder. By 2001, curious friends and would-be sleuths had posted hundreds of messages offering myriad theories on how the murder could have been perpetrated.

Van de Velde, meanwhile, continued to fight, and in December 2001, he sued the New Haven Police Department, complaining that the department had violated his civil rights by publicly citing him as the sole suspect while claiming that other individuals were also being considered. Two years later, Van de Velde added Yale as a defendant. Both suits were dismissed in March 2004. Van de Velde fought on, however, and he appealed the verdict. In April 2006, Connecticut District Court Chief Judge Robert Chatigny ruled against him. Van de Velde asked Chatigny to reconsider in May 2006. Chatigny reinstated the state claims on December 11, 2007. That suit is pending at the time of this writing.

On February 1, 2004, *Northeast* magazine published an article in which Van de Velde offered a variety of forensic possibilities. He requested that the police avail themselves of new crime-fighting technology. He encouraged investigators to review the evidence and to think "out of the box." With pen in hand, Van de Velde undertook a letter-writing campaign urging the Connecticut State Cold Case Unit to take over the case. State's attorney Michael Dearington initially refused.

By 2005, James Van de Velde had begun, at least on the surface, to reinvent himself. He had married, had a new son, and relocated to northern Maryland. His intelligence work entrenched him in one of the most puzzling cases in the nation's history: the 2001 anthrax attacks that killed five people and sickened seventeen others, casting a cloud of fear over the U.S. mail system.

Later in 2005, Donald Connery, a former reporter for *Time* and *Life* magazines and a veteran commentator on the criminal justice system, penned one of his many articles for the *Courant*. According to Connery's article, that summer, prosecutor Clark and two New Haven detectives paid a surprise visit to Van de Velde in D.C. Connery said that Clark refused to comment on the visit. He quoted Van de Velde, however: "They persuaded the Naval Criminal Intelligence Service and the Defense Security Service of the Pentagon to pull me from my post, interrogate me, demand that I take another polygraph test (despite my having passed a test two weeks earlier for a liaison post I was chosen for by the CIA), accuse me of the crime, and terminate my military assignment. As a result of Clark and the New Haven police, I was kicked out of my position as Senior Intelligence Analyst for al-Qaeda and anthrax at the Defense Intelligence Agency."

Months later, a Pentagon administrative judge and the Naval Appeals Panel restored his security clearance. Van de Velde then returned to his counterintelligence work, this time with the State Department.

For Jim Van de Velde, there seemed to be no escaping the specter of Jovin's death, nor the reality that investigators were making no headway on the case. Finally, Van de Velde's writing campaign paid off. On September 1, 2006, nearly eight years after the murder, officials transferred the investigation to the Cold Case Unit of the Chief State's Attorney's Office. In a release, state's attorney Dearington, the chief prosecutor for the office, said that the decision to transfer the case was not easy, but after eight years of investigation, the New Haven and Yale police had come no closer to making an arrest.

But the case was never added to the Cold Case Unit website, nor was there any mention of the $150,000 reward. In the subsequent weeks and months, the public learned little about the status of the case. The Cold Case Unit repeatedly refused to detail its work, and its website provided virtually nothing on Jovin or the murder.

Once again, the police's inability to show any real progress on the case piqued Van de Velde. It had now been eight years since Jovin's murder, and he still was the sole named suspect. With little recourse, Van de Velde returned to his letter-writing campaign.

And then came another glimmer of hope.

On November 29, 2007, assistant state's attorney James Clark revealed publicly—before the press and Ellen Jovin—that the Jovin case was back in the hands of the New Haven police. He then introduced the investigative team assigned to the case: Mannion, Gaffney, Wardell, and Sudol. Surely, with their combined many years of service, they could accomplish what their predecessors had not: identify Suzanne Jovin's killer. Once again, the police were making a fresh start; this time, it came nearly nine years to the day of Suzanne Jovin's death.

But was this really a fresh start for the Jovin investigative unit? Five days after the press conference, Mannion admitted in an interview with the *Yale Daily News* that he and the other three retired officers had been working on the case since the summer and had begun to collect information from telephone calls and email tip lines. So why did Clark wait until the end of November to announce the new investigative team?

Mannion said that media pressure coupled with another slew of letters from Van de Velde played a role in the fall announcement. Mannion also hoped that by tying the announcement with the anniversary of Jovin's death, it would "rekindle some memories."

Van de Velde, who continued to press the state and NHPD to use new forensic technology in the case, scoffed at the possibility that the Jovin investigative team would make any headway in the case. None of the retired officers were forensic specialists or computer forensic specialists. Neither were any of them Dr. Lee, who was still awaiting a call from the NHPD. Even Mannion admitted that this investigative "dream team" was not pursuing the case on a full-time basis. Mannion told the *Yale Daily News*: "It [the part-time status] became part of the official file, and it's something we will consider as we march down this long road."

As 2008 dawned, the Suzanne Jovin case featured more questions and incongruities than answers. For instance, what had become of the brown or tan van witnesses spotted at the crime scene at the time of the murder? Although police questioned members of the Yale faculty privately, they did not release information on the van until March 27, 2001. Why? In a release, the NHPD announced, "Witnesses have said that as they approached the corner of East Rock and Edgehill Roads, they saw a tan or brown van stopped in the roadway facing east, immediately adjacent to where Suzanne was found." On November 8 of that year, the *New Haven Register* reported that the department had "impounded a brown van as part of their Jovin investigation." To date, the department has not linked that van with the crime. Moreover, there have been no reports of witnesses seeing Jovin enter or exit any vehicle, nor has the van in question been found. Van de Velde is one of many to theorize that the killer or killers assaulted Jovin in the vehicle, and then dumped her moribund body onto the street.

Other unanswered questions concern the Fresca bottle found in the bushes near Jovin's body. Early in the investigation, police discovered the bottle bearing her fingerprints and the partial palm print of another unidentified person. But the public only became aware of the bottle on April 1, 2001, in an article written by Les Gura of the *Courant*. In December 2003, WTNH television reported what the police already knew—that there was a second pair of prints on the bottle. To date, those prints have not been identified.

More puzzling still: Where would Jovin have gotten the soda? Only Krauszer's Market on York Street near Elm Street sold Fresca at that hour. Witnesses stated, however, that Jovin was not carrying a bottle of any kind or a backpack, which could have hidden the bottle. Still, the police did not seek the store video recording of its customers from that evening; nor have they reported interviewing store employees or customers about the tragic night. Why not?

DNA taken from under Jovin's fingernails did not match that of Van de Velde, thus reducing the chances that he was the killer. Still, there was no public notice of the DNA until October 26, 2001, when New Haven police initially requested samples from Jovin's friends, family, and acquaintances, as well as rescue, police, and fire personnel at the crime scene. Police have yet to find a match for the DNA taken from under Jovin's fingernails.

Then there was Jovin's thesis on Osama bin Laden. Could al-Qaeda sympathizers have learned about the paper and exacted their revenge on Jovin?

And perhaps most important, could state, university, and local investigators have been wrong in theorizing that this was a crime of passion?

Experts suggest that the identity of Jovin's killer, and the answers to these questions, may be revealed if a witness comes forth or new technology produces additional evidence.

Perhaps old evidence could be further scrutinized and lead investigators to the identity of the killer. That's what friends and family of the late Yale coed are hoping after investigators began to look more closely at two bits of evidence during the summer of 2008. The first was the description of a man spotted running near the site where Jovin was murdered on December 4, 1998. Investigators are also looking into an unknown "someone" to whom Jovin referred in an email shortly before her death.

Lead investigator Mannion said both details had been in Jovin's case file since early in the investigation. Clark, the assistant state's attorney who is overseeing the investigation, bristled at the suggestion that police had not adequately pursued those leads.

"Don't get me started on whether the initial investigation was wonderful," Clark told the *Yale Daily News* on September 3, 2008.

"There's no way to rewrite history, so you move forward with the different focus."

Over the summer, police distributed black-and-white posters of the mysterious runner throughout East Rock. The poster read: "A physically fit, athletic looking white male with defined features, 20s to 30s years of age with well-groomed blond or dark blond hair. He was wearing dark pants and a loose fitted green jacket."

According to reports in the *New Haven Register*, the man was spotted running "as if his life depended on it" two-tenths of a mile from the murder scene. The July 2 *Hartford Courant* reported that a Hamden woman provided police with the man's description after he raced by her car, shortly before 10 P.M. After interviewing her, police took the woman to Van de Velde's office to see if she would identify him as the runner. She did not.

Another potential suspect—the "someone" Jovin referred to in her email—also lacks an identity. Jovin wrote the email at 9:02 P.M. on December 4, 1998, from her Park Street apartment and sent it to a female classmate. Jovin said that she had her classmate's GRE study materials, but admitted that she had loaned them to "someone" else. The identity of that someone else remains a mystery, however—just another element in the conundrum that is the Suzanne Jovin murder.

If anyone has further information on what may have happened that night, the Jovin investigation team can be directly contacted by phone at (203) 676-1575 or by email at jovincase@gmail.com.

CHAPTER 8

Three Strikes and You're Out?

✳ ✳ ✳

On a cloudless evening in late September 2007, Dr. William Petit Jr. stood before a somber audience of friends, family, and neighbors packed into the stands of a Cheshire, Connecticut, ball field. Behind him and to the left of the podium stood large, framed photos of his late wife and two daughters. Petit's face was drawn, reflecting the pain that lingered from the July 23 triple murder of Petit's forty-eight-year-old wife, Jennifer Hawke-Petit, and daughters Hayley, seventeen, and Michaela, eleven.

His address to the crowd of more than a thousand at Maclary Athletic Complex marked Petit's first public comments since home invaders brutally murdered his wife and children, savagely beat him, and set the family's home on fire. Charged with the murders and a string of related crimes were, as Dr. Petit dubbed them, "Satan personified": twenty-seven-year-old Joshua Komisarjevsky and forty-four-year-old Steven Hayes of Winsted. The alleged killers were veteran cat burglars, free on probation at the time of the murders.

The *New Haven Register* captured the emotion and depth of Petit's feelings: "Cheshire's children that are still here, please know that you are important. We need you to help us to be a better Cheshire, a more moral Connecticut, and a better United States of America." He added, "Satan personified, evil on earth destroyed all that is good in my life."

The memorial service featured Petit's comments plus hymns sung by an ecumenical choir composed of members of all of Cheshire's churches. Petit's Sorghum Mill Drive neighbors lent their remembrances to the two-hour service. Chris Rao, who was especially close to Jennifer Hawke-Petit, called her "a mother to us all."

If Mrs. Hawke-Petit was the neighborhood matriarch, the entire Petit family symbolized the heart and soul of a community known for togetherness, and not capital crime. Simply put, to those who knew them, the Petit family embodied all that was and is good in humanity. Mrs. Hawke-Petit was a nurse and codirector of the health center at Cheshire Academy, a respected boarding school, before being diagnosed with multiple sclerosis a decade ago. At the time of her death, she was active in the Connecticut state chapter of the MS Society. Her daughters, Hayley and Michaela, also were active in the program. Hayley, who had planned to attend Dartmouth College in 2008, had been an on-air spokesperson for WTNH television during fund-raising activities for the MS Society. Michaela expressed the desire to follow in Hayley's footsteps. Dr. Petit was a prominent endocrinologist and medical director of the Joslin Diabetes Center Affiliate at the Hospital of Central Connecticut in New Britain.

To the residents of this open-door community of twenty-nine thousand, located twenty minutes from Waterbury and half an hour from New Haven, the question even today remains obvious: Why would anyone wish to destroy the lives of one family?

Lieutenant Jay Markella, Cheshire police spokesman, told the *Waterbury Republican-American*: "It's by far the worst thing any of us have ever seen."

Police investigations and reports underscore the horror of the crimes. The state medical examiner confirmed that all three women were raped, and Mrs. Hawke-Petit had been strangled, while her daughters died of smoke inhalation. The girls were tied to their beds and then left to die after perpetrators doused their rooms with gasoline and ignited it. Dr. Petit had been beaten with a baseball bat, thrown down the stairs, and tied up in the cellar. Despite his severe injuries, the doctor escaped from the burning house.

According to sources close to the investigation, the suspects followed Michaela and her mother home from a shopping trip to the supermarket. They then went to Wal-Mart around 9 A.M. to purchase an air rifle and rope, part of a plan to burgle the Petit home.

In a move almost as bizarre as the crimes themselves, the suspects then followed Mrs. Hawke-Petit to a local bank and forced her to make a $15,000 withdrawal. A bank employee called the police around 9:30 A.M. According to the *Hartford Courant*, bank employees refused to give Hawke-Petit the money. She then informed them that she and her family were being held hostage. One of the suspects was waiting for Hawke-Petit outside the bank. On the way back to the Petit home, one of the suspects purchased a can of gasoline, according to the *Waterbury Republican-American*.

Even before the crime was committed, numerous witnesses had spotted the suspects. When Cheshire police were dispatched to the Petit home at 300 Sorghum Mill Drive, they found the house on fire. The suspects raced off the property in one of the Petits' vehicles, slammed into three police cruisers, and were arrested a block from the house.

Jennifer Hawke-Petit was found dead on the first floor. Hayley lay deceased at the head of the stairs. Michaela was bound to her bed and burned almost beyond recognition by the fire. Meanwhile, a badly beaten Dr. Petit had dragged himself to a neighbor's house.

The horrific nature of the crimes has affected the town and the state unlike many murders in state history. The murders underscore how vulnerable people are, regardless of their place of residence. In the wake of the home invasion, folks throughout the state have become more cognizant of locking their homes and cars and have purchased equipment to protect their safety.

The Petit murders also opened the eyes of the state legislators. Shortly after the killings, Governor M. Jodi Rell ordered a top-to-bottom review of the criminal justice system to see how it had failed. In the case of the Petit family, the Connecticut justice system had failed because of its laws regarding parole and the overcrowding of its prisons, vis-à-vis a shrinking state budget.

How could two men who already had a lengthy record of burglary and larceny be walking the streets? The answer: Neither had a history of violent crimes. Each had more than twenty burglaries on his record. At the time of the murders, both were free on parole after serving prison time for burglary convictions in 2003. Both were assigned to a halfway house in Hartford before being released on parole. In Connecticut, prisoners "may be released from confinement and receive parole after serving more than half of their sentences."

During their July 2007 arraignment, Komisarjevsky was charged with one count each of assault, aggravated sexual assault, burglary, conspiracy to commit arson, robbery compounded with risk of injury to a minor, two counts of larceny, and four counts of kidnapping—all in the first degree. Hayes was charged with most of the same crimes, including sexual assault.

The case underscored the challenges the Rell administration faced—and still faces—concerning the judicial system.

In late 2007, state legislators began the difficult process of changing the state's criminal laws. The judicial committee heard testimony on some fifteen proposals to better counter violent crime. At the heart of the crime reform effort was the state's Repeat Offender Law, known commonly as the "three strikes" law. It would send criminals to prison for life if convicted of three violent felonies.

Home invasions would be reclassified as violent felonies, and a conviction would count as one strike under the proposed law.

Opponents argued that such an approach could limit a judge's discretion in sentencing, or that it might undermine rehabilitation programs, which are needed when most prisoners are eventually going to return to society.

Other suggested options included a full-time parole board, whose members would earn $90,000 per year plus benefits worth another $55,000. Another Democratic plan called for $110 million appropriated for a thousand-bed prison and another $150 million for a twelve-hundred-bed prison for inmates with mental problems.

After months of debate, in April 2008, both the Connecticut Senate and House of Representatives passed a revamped persistent offender bill as a response to the Petit home invasion of July 2007. The House passed the bill by a resounding 128 to 12. The proposal included $10 million in additional funding to "hire more prosecutors, public defenders, state police, parole officers and GPS tracking of offenders living in the community."

The new proposal was a streamlined version of the law favored by Governor Rell, who wanted a "three-strikes-and-you're-out" bill. Under that proposal, "a repeat violent offender would automatically be sentenced to life in prison without possibility of release, after committing a third violent felony." The bill passed by the House and Senate is designed to make sure violent crime repeaters stay off the streets. Crime repeaters will receive double penalties for a second violent offense, and third-time offenders will see their penalties tripled.

In early May, Rell signed a criminal justice package that included the repeat offender bill approved by the House and Senate. The passage of the bill into law will not salve Dr. William Petit's pain, but it will help Connecticut residents feel safer in their homes.

Bibliography

Publications

Bulletin of the Connecticut Academy of Science and Engineering 19, no. 2 (Summer 2004).

Connecticut Law Tribune.

Lee, Dr. Henry C., and Thomas W. O'Neill. *Cracking More Cases: The Forensic Science of Solving Crimes.* New York: Prometheus Books, 2004.

McConnell, Virginia A. *Arsenic under the Elms.* Westport, CT. Praeger, 1999. Reprint. Nebraska: University of Nebraska Press, 2005.

Websites

www.judiciary.senate.gov
www.truecrime.com
www.amazon.com
www.cnn.com
www.hartfordcourant.com
www.newhavenregister.com
www.newyorktimes.com
www.vanityfair.com

www.SpotCrime.com
www.cbs.com
www.courttv.com
www.usnews.com
www.foxnews.com
www.ct.gov
www.yaledailynews.com
www.crimelibrary.com

Newspapers

Greenwich Time
Hartford Courant
Meriden Record-Journal
New Haven Register